Morelle Smith's poetry and prose has been published in journals and anthologies in the UK, Europe and North America, including *New Writing Scotland*, *Times Literary Supplement*, *La Traductière*, *Culture and Cosmos*, *Crannog* and *Balkan Travellers*. Her work has won prizes and awards from UK and Canadian magazines and her poetry has been displayed on transport systems in Edinburgh and Glasgow. She has lived and worked in various parts of Europe and her writing has been translated into several European languages including French, Albanian and Romanian. Online publications can be found on her blog http://rivertrain.blogspot.co.uk

D1613300

Tirana Papers

Morelle Smith

Kairos

First published 2013 by Kairos

© Morelle Smith 2013

ISBN: 978-0-9552896-9-9

The author's right to be identified as author of this book under the Copyright, Designs and Patents Act 1988 has been asserted.

Printed in the UK by Bell & Bain Ltd., Glasgow

The paper used in this book is recyclable. It is made from low chlorine pulps produced in a low energy, low emissions manner from renewable forests.

The author benefited from a Writer's Residency
at the Monastery of Saorge, Centre des Monuments
Nationaux, France, for the completion of this book.

Also by Morelle Smith

The Star Reaper
Deepwater Terminal
Streets of Tirana, Almost Spring
The Way Words Travel
The Ravens and the Lemon Tree
Time Loop
Gold Tracks, Fallen Fruit

To Frieda and Matti

Contents

Introduction

Albania – a country that had recently emerged from almost half a century of Stalinist communism, a country that the outside world knew little of, for its rulers preferred to keep it locked inside a near-hermetic seal of silence. The killings and incarcerations only became known once the regime fell in 1990 and people started to leave, often by night, in overcrowded boats. A few years later, in 1997, the collapse of the Pyramid Schemes meant that the majority of the population, who had sunk their savings into these investments, lost everything, and their anger and despair turned to looting – firstly of an arms depot, followed by a wave of destruction. Government and municipal buildings, associated with the hated political regime, were stormed, ransacked and pillaged. There was shooting and rioting in the streets.

Two years later, in 1999, refugees from Kosova poured over borders and many of them came to Albania. The Kosovars were homeless, fleeing from soldiers, burned out houses, rape and murder of their families, exhausted, frightened and hungry. Albanians opened their doors. Over half of the refugees were taken into people's homes.

When the aid workers and international relief organisations moved into the countries bordering on Kosova to assist with the huge numbers of refugees, it quickly became apparent that this host country was in a state of dilapidation and in some cases, extreme poverty. The physical infrastructure was like an old coat that had been patched and repaired so many times it was coming apart in several places at once. Much of the population was armed and underground crime was becoming rapidly organised and profitable. The social fabric was as ripped and trampled on as the physical one and the country was having the equivalent of a mental breakdown or a psychotic episode.

When I arrived in early 2000 Albania looked as if it was living in the debris of an explosion. Aid was starting to come into the country and the beginnings of repair and reconstruction were being made. The atmosphere was still suspicious and volatile, but at least for some, a sense of hope was beginning to filter through.

The time I spent in Albania in 2000 saw the beginnings of real change. Schools hospitals and train stations were being renovated, water pipes repaired, trees planted, roads resurfaced, covered market places built and training programmes for teachers and public health workers were initiated. It was an extraordinary time. And of course, no matter how many projects went ahead there were still many more that could not be completed because the funding was limited.

In many ways Albania has changed a lot since then. The new airport is spacious, glass-fronted, full of reflected light. Tirana's population has almost doubled, the city centre is full of new buildings, shiny banks, smart restaurants and shops. The main roads are now well surfaced and sleek coaches take you comfortably from one town to the next, where you can stay in top notch expensive hotels. Although few Albanians of course, can afford them.

The cost of living has soared and in rural areas there is still great poverty, while the political situation, though turbulent, is more stable than it used to be.

But this memoir is of the country as I experienced it, just coming out of a time of immense turmoil. For decades Albanians had hardly ever seen any foreigners and even if they did catch sight of the few visitors who passed through, they were not allowed to speak to them unless it was a prearranged and state controlled event. Suddenly, foreigners were all over the place. No wonder they stared at us!

With the Albatross we
Enter Mythological Time

Time [in the Balkans] is understood
mythologically rather than chronologically.
Paul Mojzes: *Yugoslavian Inferno*

1

The airport bus was crowded. Two people close to me spoke in low voices and the rest of us stood there, holding onto the black plastic straps and the little scraps of identity we carry with us from one time-zone to another, one airport to another, enabling us to know where we're going when we arrive in the next airport, even if we've never seen it before. Sometimes you even know who you will meet – everything has coherence and a reassuring sense of continuity.

I looked ahead, at the approaching terminal lights.

Athens airport is like a bus station, the woman in the plane had said, really not very comfortable. But if you want somewhere to stay, there's a hotel just five minutes away. Don't take a taxi, it's really quicker to walk. Go out of the airport, turn right, it's just a block away, the first hotel you come to. Called The Albatross.

I had slipped out of my past life though its memories

accompanied me of course. The past is gone as soon as we turn our head and face another direction, but while we usually assume that the same people and the same places will re-appear tomorrow and the next day, some pasts are packed and put away with care and attention and the knowledge of distance and separation. Sometimes this is your choice and sometimes it is not.

At the terminal building people collected their luggage and disappeared. The darkness outside seemed to take their solidity and melt it immediately. Or perhaps their continuity preserved them from the worst of the night's dissolving capacities, soft dark hands shaping you into its own fantasies.

It was 3.30 in the morning. I found a place that sold coffee and asked about the Albatross Hotel. I was told that it was very close, confirming the woman's directions. I put the big rucksack on my back and the small one I used as hand-luggage, on my front. I walked out of the terminal building, into the deserted car park.

In completely strange circumstances, memories are simply mute witnesses. They watch, wide-eyed, amazed. I wondered if they really did assist, in some invisible way that I was unaware of. It could be possible, I thought, perhaps they smoothed the sheets before I lay down on the bed. Perhaps they stroked my hair and sang me lullabies to drown out the throbbing in the head that you only begin to hear, after flying, in the quiet of your hotel room, when all other external sounds disappear. But how these memories could connect with the future, I had no idea. Simple enough steps had brought me to this moment, in a hotel room in Athens, with the night already past its deepest and darkest, a short night, before I went on to the next stage of the journey.

Perhaps the steps were not as simple as they appeared. In fact, I knew they were not, but the visible, external process, like jewellery on a dancer, is what catches the eye and draws us into the dance too, lured in by some desire, some promise, our jackdaw senses I thought, hooked on what glitters, hooked on reflected light.

A few months before, I'd made a trip to Italy, which prised me out of my life, scooped me out like a spoonful of ripe melon. It woke up an incurable restlessness. Then I'd met Ted, when I was working in the sorting office, helping out with the Christmas mail. In the chilly December nights we'd slip outside into the loading bay to smoke a cigarette. That's when I got talking to Ted. His parents were involved with aid work in the Balkans and he was able to give me an email address that might be useful.

No harm in contacting them, he said. So I did.

My name was passed to another organisation, which offered me work in Tirana. A few weeks later, in February, I left Edinburgh for Albania.

On the bus out to the airport it began to snow. The London flight was indefinitely delayed because of the bad weather which meant I missed my connection. It was late in the evening before I finally left Heathrow and boarded an Olympic plane to Athens. As we pulled back from the departure point someone was framed in the window, standing, watching.

The plane moved slowly past the green string of the runway lights, then speeded up and leaped forward. A sea of golden jewels was spread out beneath us, little beads of light on intricate strings. Then they were gone, disappeared, all these looping threads, like aboriginal dream-time patterns. They reappeared on the other side of clouds – greyish light shrugging across the golden bead-work. Gaps now, in the skin of light, dark places, shadow places, part of the land that slept. The lights became ragged streamers, then wisps, memories of light.

2

A thunderous banging noise woke me up. I thought the building was being shelled. It was just beginning to get light and I looked around the room, grabbing at any visual clues to tell me where I was.

Once the roaring pounding noise that shook the building had moved off into distance and the pace of my heart-beat had slowed a little, I remembered where I was. In the Albatross Hotel in Athens, very close to the airport. The building was not being shelled after all. It was just an aircraft taking off a few metres away. The next time it happened, though it woke me up, I was less alarmed and soon fell asleep again. As I did after the third time and the fourth.

In the morning I have a shower and go out on the balcony. There's a view of palm trees, and a hill with those precise folds lovingly smoothed by some sculptor. Nearby are a few houses, separated by a handful of trees. On a flat roof dotted with green plants someone is hanging out her washing. The air is filled with the sound of noisy birds and the sun is shining in a clear blue sky.

In the large downstairs lobby there's the albatross, with its huge wings and yellow beak with its downward hook at the end. I feel uneasy with the name. Too many associations with the Ancient Mariner's fated, seeming inexplicable relationship with such a bird. I want to erase it, change it, make it different. I want to go back in time and love the bird, stroke its huge wings, close my eyes and put my face against its beak. I stroke the feathers which have the softness of water.

The girl who gives me coffee says that the bird's wingspan is three metres but she does not know where it came from or how it got there. And the parrot's name (there's a parrot in a cage) is Rikki. They think it's cold here just now but as I walk back to the airport it feels like a day in early summer in Scotland, a day in May.

At that point I begin to wonder if it is such a simple thing, future following on from past. Perhaps it's not the future I'm going on into at all, perhaps I'm going back into the past, not the past I know, but a different one. Like going back to change what had happened once and bring the albatross back to life.

In Athens airport men in grey trousers and sleeveless jumpers were walking about, carrying streamers of lottery tickets no-one ever seems to buy.

A broad-shouldered woman with close-cropped hair frisked me before I got on the plane from Athens to Tirana. There was an atmosphere here I did not quite understand. There was suspicion, mistrust, a subtle accusation on the one side. And defensiveness, a mixture of anger and sullen acceptance on the other.

The flight was just over an hour long. All I could see from the window was ridge after ridge of brown mountains. The Master Painter had flicked his brush over them, so the peaks were dotted and smeared with white. Crossing another time zone, we landed five minutes after we had left Greece.

3

In the immigration area in Rinas airport, Albania, there are two queues – FOR ALBANIAN CITIZENS and FOR FOREING CITIZENS. A policeman stands between the two lines of 'foreing' nationals. A man in the queue says something to him and the policeman takes his passport, puts it in the window in front of the immigration official, so he jumps the queue. As he moves forward past the others still waiting in line, the man hands the policemen some notes, which he pockets.

Perception, in a new place, is patchy and hazy. It's almost as if the eyes cannot really see, until the visual information is linked together through meaning. Until that happens, the eyes grab at details and hang on, like a painter putting blobs of colour here, an outline there. The picture builds up slowly into a large canvas that then gives the impression of always having been there, waiting to be revealed. But on the way to Tirana from Rinas airport. I only saw the colourful blobs that stood out. The landscape was almost flat, only becoming rounded as we approached the city. So much empty land and only a few houses here and there, many incomplete, red bricks and red tiled roofs. Litter at the roadside, mainly pink and blue plastic bags. A few people were walking along the road, sometimes with a cow or a couple of sheep a, primrose yellow mosque just before we turn off from the road to Durres, and headed inland to Tirana. The huge sky shed light with the same generosity that I found in Greece. Tirana is on the last outpost of plain, backed up against the mountains, which are moody, unpredictable, alternately protective and intimidating.

I'd been picked up at the airport by two of my future colleagues, one of them driving the white four by four with the NGO logo on the side. I would be sharing a flat with them, they would see to it that I settled in, they would answer any questions I had.

4

When I look out of the window of my apartment I see a construction worker on the building opposite, standing on a jutting stone outcrop, a little ledge, three storeys up. He leans over to catch a bucket being winched up. There is nothing to break his fall.

The short-cut to work only takes about fifteen minutes, winding through back streets and alleyways. I pass street sellers with boxes of brightly coloured fruit piled in front of them, and the little cafés where dark-haired men can be seen clustered round tables from early in the morning.

The side streets are covered in mud. As soon as I step out of the apartment block onto what is no more than a dirt track, I have to negotiate large puddles and potholes. On the main roads, there are often gaping holes and broken flagstones. This presents a danger at night, as there are no street lights, only lights from windows and the occasional illuminated sign.

The mud also mixes with the rubbish. There are large garbage bins in the city, but these are emptied infrequently. Stray dogs and cats prowl around the overflowing bins. Miscellaneous rubbish drifts in the street and accumulates in piles – in vacant ground between buildings, or on the muddy side streets. Garbage on the main streets is usually burned. Sometimes the rubbish bins are set alight and obscured by dark acrid smoke.

The river Lana bisects the town. It is almost always a dark-brown sludge colour. The Aussies call it 'crappy creek'. On one of the side streets a water pipe disgorges water, constantly. It looks a lot clearer than the brown colour of the river, but no-one seems inclined to plug it up or divert it somewhere else where it might be more useful. Every day water pours out onto the street. Children float makeshift boats made out of old plastic containers, on the pool this water provides.

I work on the second floor of a three-storey building which is rented by IRC (International Rescue Committee), in the Rruga Mujo Ulqinaku. The staircase is open, though covered by a roof. From the balcony on the third floor there is a view out over rooftops and tiny garden areas. The roof-tiles are irregular, bleached pale pink by the sun, and the yards are mainly filled with planks of wood and scrawny trees. Behind the houses the mountains rise up suddenly. This morning there were thin rivulets of white trailing a short distance down the mountainsides. The sky is clear blue and the sun is bright, dazzling light, and warm. The balustrade around the balcony is very low so I move away from the edge and don't look down, but look out and up, the foreground a tangle of tiles. Smooth-sculpted, pressed and folded mountains are draped like curtains along the backdrop.

Most of the Albanian drivers who work with us have degrees. Eryon is an artist and Frederic is a musician. Gramoz has a geology degree and is now studying law. One person who has just been employed as a Field Officer is a doctor, but she cannot get work here. There is immense local talent, but no jobs – or, if jobs, they earn between $70 and $100 per month. So George, an Australian in charge of Operations, warns against leaving a big tip in restaurants. The waiters, he says, are mostly students and if they make too much money waiting tables they'll drop out of university. I ponder the logic of this.

When I first met George he briefed me about general safety. If I was ever in any trouble I was to get in touch with him immediately, no matter what time of day or night.

But you'd be best, he said, not to go anywhere on your own.

Driving at night, apart from in the city itself, was forbidden, because of the danger of bandits. Certain areas of the country, such as the remote and mountainous north, were also out of bounds as our safety could not be guaranteed. Even walking in the city at night was discouraged because of the lack of street lights, and to do so on one's own, particularly for a woman, was foolhardy in the extreme. I was reminded that the country had only recently emerged from anarchy and a large proportion of the population was armed. Gunfire could be heard at night sometimes and even daytime shootings were not uncommon.

I understood the need for safety yet Tirana did not feel like a dangerous place to me. The only thing I found a little unsettling was the quiet of the streets, as soon as one left the brightly lit restaurants in the central area. The streets were dark and deserted and the few times I disobeyed advice and walked home on my own, the silence and the darkened windows felt unnerving and I felt relief once I'd reached my apartment and turned the key four times in the lock to open the door.

5

During the night, there is a thunderstorm and heavy rain. In the morning, roads are awash. In some parts of town the traffic inches along in water that reaches half-way up their wheels, brown wakes parting on either side.

What wonderful weather, my flatmate Susan says delightedly, gazing rapturously out of the window. Lightning flashes and thunder grumbles. Susan is from Townsville Australia, where apparently it never rains.

The power fails a couple of times in the morning but it's unlikely to be due to the weather, as this is a daily occurrence. Because of voltage regulators and a UPS (interrupted power supply) on my machine, I have a few seconds' grace in which to save the material that's being worked on before the computer screen goes blank. But the constant power failures have wreaked such havoc on the computers that the UPS is known as 'Useless Piece of Shit'.

Later in the morning I go with Steve and Rudina from the Psycho-Social sector, to Kruje, about an hour's drive from Tirana. We are going to check that a training session, funded by IRC, is going ahead without any problems. The training is being given to doctors and nurses working in the public health sector, and is related to awareness and treatment of Post Traumatic Stress Disorder. This is relevant both to refugees and to those who suffered torture under the communist regime.

The land is flat on the road to Kruje. There are many semi-constructed houses of dark red brick. The road is full of potholes. There are a few walls, mainly in front of fairly sumptuous-looking houses. Otherwise, the fields just begin at the sides of the road. Many of them are waterlogged this morning. We pass through a small town, Fush-Kruje, with pavement stalls selling fruit, vegetables, large plastic bins, hoses, car parts. Some of the stalls have makeshift plastic coverings over them. As we leave the town behind, the road begins to climb. The river in the valley below us is a garish orange-brown colour as if it had been dyed, but could perhaps have come from the mud that's been washed into it, by the rain. The earth is a rich reddish-brown. Kruje is built on a mountainside, and a winding road leads up to it. This road has a couple of small rivers running through it this morning. Its streets are lined with trees – a variety of pine, with trailing, feathery needles, and other trees that look like willow.

After the meeting, we go down the little cobbled street to the old bazaar area, where the shops have wooden frontages and awnings. Sculptures, jewellery and carpets are shown in the windows and bags, scarves and other pieces of material hang outside. The carpets are woven in traditional designs, with colourful patterns.

We have lunch in a little restaurant with a low wooden ceiling. The wooden chairs all have sheepskins on them, but this doesn't do much to alleviate the cold. There is no heating and the chill from the rain and mist penetrates our many layers of clothes.

6

The clouds had moved in all day, like barges freighted with goatskins of rain, dropping their cargo over the city as they rolled like tanks in from the sea, heading for the mountains. When I left work the rain was still falling, mingling with the evening murk, splashing across buildings like the work of a despairing painter, gathering in spreading puddles across the lane. I was picking my way across a thin strip of mud that wound between the puddles, when Olga came up behind me.

You don't have an umbrella, she said, like a stern schoolteacher.

Well no, I said meekly.

Olga took my arm and moved her umbrella so that it covered us both.

But you must get one, she said. This weather is so dreadful, you cannot walk around without one. You must walk with me.

We skirted the puddles that almost covered the Rruga Mujo Ulqinaku, negotiated the debris-covered slope at the end and went through the hole in the wall, through the entrance to the block of flats, and came out in Rruga Myslym Shyri. We walked up to the corner, turned right onto Sami Frasheri and continued along the bridge over the river.

Olga explained where she lived, but my inner map of Tirana was still very small and I could not picture it. I hesitated at the bridge. This wasn't the route I'd taken before.

I think I know where I am, I said.

I will come with you, Olga said

I tried to protest that it was taking her out of her way but she had a calm authority about her that made me feel like a lost child, both hapless and relieved.

Our heads were close together, under the umbrella. Olga's fair hair was pulled back from her face and her light-brown eyes glistened in the gloom of the falling rain and the hungry night, that fastened on the streets like a predator, with matted fur and claws exposed. Olga's wide eyes, prominent jaw-bone and delicately pointed chin looked abruptly sad as if a flare of rain had passed over her and the memory had soaked into her bone structure, leaving a damp trail of wistfulness, like evening smoke from distant chimneys.

Will you know how to get back from here? I asked.

Of course. I have been here two months, I know my way around. But you have been here two days only – so, it is confusing at first.

Do you live on your own?

I share an apartment with Jean-Paul, my partner. He works for the UN. Would you like to come round tomorrow afternoon? I've asked Steve and Susan as well – they will tell you where our apartment is.

Thank you, I said.

I recognised the immobilised white Citroen, but after that, I was not sure which turn off to take. There were no street lights and off the main road, no streets either, just uneven areas with puddle-filled hollows. No lights in the shops and kiosks, because of the constant power cuts. Just one or two candles burning, feeble gleams in the darkness. We turned off down a muddy path but it became unfamiliar, so we went back to the main road. At the entrance to the second path, I said, It must be this one, I'll be OK now. But Olga was having none of it.

I'll come with you, until you are certain she said. We picked our way through the puddles of the muddy lane until I recognised the gates at the entrance to the apartment block.

This is it. Definitely.

You are sure? You are all right?

Something about her poise, that whiff of sadness and her brisk protectiveness, threw a glow over the sodden path and the utter darkness of the street lined with ugly concrete apartment blocks.

I'm fine. Thanks again. See you tomorrow.

I walked over to the gate and glanced over my shoulder, before going in. I saw a black blur disappearing back round the corner. I walked quickly across the little yard and unlocked the main door.

7

There are frequent power cuts. At the office, you get into the habit of regularly saving your work on the computer and at home you make sure that you always know the location of the matches and candles. In the apartment where I live there are two varieties of power cuts, one where the whole block is affected and another that's confined to the apartment. The latter is caused by having the washing machine and heater on at the same time – or washing machine and stove. It's easily remedied, by going downstairs and flicking on the trip-switch then turning off one of the offending electrical appliances. But if the whole block is affected, you simply have to light the candles and sit it out.

I share the apartment in Rruga Emin Duraku with Susan and Steve, from Townsville, Australia. Steve keeps a small bag packed beside his bed, containing essential items, in case of an earthquake. He tells me of the quickest escape route to safety, that he has devised. It involves jumping from the balcony of their room.

He says they also have a plan of what to do in the event of a tsunami hitting the coast of Australia. Also, he says, the Aborigines are moving inland, which may be a more definite sign of imminent catastrophe. But Rupert, another co-worker, says that people in earthquake-prone countries build with that in mind.

It's important for buildings to be flexible in an earthquake, he says.

Rupert tells us he has been in two earthquakes, one in Tibet and another in Romania. The one in Tibet happened at night. He was asleep, he said, and was dreaming that a large person was outside the building, shaking it and demanding money from him!

Steve's other fears, apart from earthquakes, are – sudden outbreaks of violence (shootings), narrow unlit roads (mud tracks) at night, Serbian troops invading Kosova (which means his leave will be cancelled as he and Susan are booked to go to England in a few days time), and dying of a heart attack.

It's happened to people younger than me he says, quite seriously. When I ask him how old he is he says on his birthday in April, he'll be thirty. Steve's background is air-force, then working with Aboriginal street children for several years before training as a psychologist. He has a big heart, with constricted external access (or so I feel) and frustration can build up quickly. He tends to be initially suspicious of people and their motives, or so he claims. When we started teasing each other and he made some derogatory comments about me I realised that it was his Antipodean sense of humour, which meant that he accepted me.

8

Saturday. My first week-end in Tirana. My first walk
on my own. From the apartment block I turned left and
followed the usual route to work. For the first part, you
skirt the mud and puddles and then come out onto the
busy corner crowded with fruit and vegetable sellers.

You then cross the Boulevard Bajram Curri and
continue over a pedestrian footbridge across the river. You
come out onto another street, whose name I have not yet
learned, turn right for a few yards, then cross. A landmark
on this street is a dirty cream Citroen car which always
sits there – it's got a completely flat front tyre. If that car
is ever moved I could get very confused. Just up from the
flat-tyre car is a garage and you turn left there, past the
broken pipe that always gushes out water. This is another
muddy path and at the further end, there's a rubbish heap
where a rooster and a couple of hens peck disconsolately.

At the end of this path is a shop with fancy squares of
curved and frosted glass – another useful landmark. I turn
left there for a few yards and cross the street at the 'hole
in the wall' so called because the wall used to be solid, but
the residents apparently got tired of having to walk a long
way round and, somehow or other, they made a hole in
the wall that they could get through. This was bricked up,
but the hole reappeared. There is now a formal door-way,
cemented in stone to prove that the 'hole in the wall' is a
real and recognised access – a genuine right of way. On
the other side you come out onto Rruga Mujo Ulqinaku
where the IRC offices are – almost immediately opposite a
new apartment block whose walls are painted bright blue.

Further along the street, which is really another muddy

track, only just wide enough for two cars to pass, with perhaps a pedestrian or two flattened against the walls, a little cart comes along, pulled by a pony. The driver sits at the front and two or three sheep are in the back.

I come out onto the Rruga Kavaje and turn right. The traffic is very heavy and the air full of exhaust fumes. The closer you get to the town centre, the more people sound their horns. Right-of-way is never very obvious and crossing the road, as a pedestrian, gets more and more hazardous. There are a few traffic lights but these are not very closely observed. Policemen direct the traffic at some of the busier intersections. Crossing the street is definitely an art-form, I decide. It's got something to do with bluff and bravura, a mixture of insolence and what looks like a disregard for the joys and benefits of corporeal existence. At least it looks like that to me. Nobody runs to get out of the way of oncoming traffic (except me). Running, or even walking briskly, is probably the most despised behaviour possible. But I've a feeling it's going to take me some time before I can affect the bold, insolent, pause, saunter, swerve and just-keep-going attitude of the local pedestrians.

Madeleine Allbright, the US Secretary of State, made an official visit to Tirana. Her mission was to thank the people of Albania for their generosity and hospitality to the Kosovar refugees the year before. The main streets in the town centre were hung with flags, both US and Albanian. We walked down the wide boulevard past the Rogner Hotel where she was staying. The street was full of police vans and we passed a couple of soldiers with Kalashnikovs. On the other side of the street were another two, wearing wide capes which made them look like dark bats. There were a couple of caped men on top of the roof as well. TV cameras were set up opposite the hotel entrance. We stood and waited for a while. A young woman came out, the cameras were switched on and she talked into the microphone.

Steve was convinced that a distant hammering noise was gunfire. I thought it sounded like someone banging in nails.

Someone's building a garden shed, I said. Steve pointed at me and said to Dave, our American Health Officer – listen to that, that's called denial.

And we all laughed and shuffled our feet and stuck our hands into coat pockets, for it was cold and the lowering clouds looked as if it could rain at any moment. Steve said there was no way that Madeleine Allbright was going to walk out of those gates for there was not nearly enough security. He turned out to be right. When the TV people started packing up, we left as well.

There weren't any cars here during the communist regime, said Dave. Or hardly any. Only the *nomenklatura*, the big shots, the political elite, had cars. You look at pictures taken then and there were no cars on the streets. But now – there's all these cars, everyone's got cars, but how can they afford them on the money they make here? Look at all these Mercedes. Almost all the cars you see here, they're stolen. People go into Germany...

And he then launched into a long explanation of how the cars were stolen, which included crossing borders and changing number-plates.

We were walking past the US Embassy. What used to be the entrance is now blocked off with sandbags and the high walls are topped with coils of razor wire. But past the Embassy you go on into the residential part of town. Here there are large detached houses, with gardens surrounded by high walls with entrance gates.

*

Almost everything I experienced here was new, sights, sounds, even tastes and smells, and certainly the people that I spent time with. It was almost as if my present held no memories. Since everything was new, there was no sense of repetition and the people and their gestures and the way they spoke, all had this air of openness about them, a kind of see-through quality which I found exhilarating. It was liberating too, for these people knew nothing of me and of my past and so had no bank of preconceptions to fall back on.

My past identity did not exist in this new place, among these people. I had no reputation to uphold, no history had gone before me, no successes to live up to, no failures to confess.

What in everyday life comes to seem familiar and banal, was a source of fascination for me because it was so different. When you see things for the first time, it's as if your perceptions have been rinsed. You do not know how things link together, what interpretations to put on anything. You do not judge, divide perceptions into good or bad, you just absorb, enthralled at the differentness of what your life has turned into.

Everything was fascinating, brushed with vigour and late winter sun.

9

Fier lies about a hundred kilometres south of Tirana, but because the roads are in such a state of disrepair it takes about three hours to drive there. I go with Chris and Ira, the Education and Community Development team and we leave at seven in the morning. The road is full of potholes, so Frederic, the driver, weaves from one side to the other in an effort to avoid them. We pass several small carts, pulled by ponies. One small pony walks along slowly, with a large man sitting side-saddle on a bulging sack. Some of the fields have makeshift fences made of rusted metal sheets.

Dangling scarecrows, teddy bears or other soft toys, including one large toy parrot, are tied to corrugated tin in front of buildings under construction, or on the wooden scaffolding itself. I ask Ira about them and she says that they are put there by superstitious people to ward off 'the Bad Eye' especially on new buildings. I also ask her about the small grey edifices that are scattered all over the fields. They have smooth round tops and look like mushrooms or homes for dwarves. She tells me they are bunkers, built during the communist regime, against the threat of invasion. All of the Western countries, she said ironically, were bound to be so jealous of us that invasion was imminent of course, and we had to be prepared. The truth, regarding the attitude of Western European countries towards Albania, was rather different. I later read in Miranda Vickers' *Albania* that the real and more valid fear was of invasion by Russia, after Hoxha, the communist dictator, split with that country.

In Durres, we drive past the NATO army base, a fenced in area containing row after row of KFOR Jeeps and trucks. There's also a motorway and bridge under construction, and a kiosk selling food is wedged between the partially built motorway and a rubbish dump.

As we drive from Durres to Lushnija, we pass a wood of pines on a small hill. The railway runs just beside the road. A cow skull is perched on one of the metal reinforcement rods sticking out of a building under construction. On a detour from the road, we drive onto a dirt track which passes slopes of olive trees.

Lushnija's wide main street is lined with palms. But on the outskirts of the town, we pass large abandoned buildings. Every single window is broken. As we enter Fier, we pass a row of kiosks which are like large metal beach huts. There are palm trees here too and some very ornate houses with big windows and wide balconies.

Our first visit in Fier is to the Naim Frasheri School, named after Albania's most famous poet, the Director, Asgesi Musa, tells us. The fact that he does not have enough money to buy for the school library the books of the writer the school is named after, is only one of the results of chronic underfunding. They have not been able to buy any new books for the library for ten years but compared with other schools they are fortunate to have a library at all, he says. Other results of lack of funding are much more obvious. The little room where we are sitting has holes in the wall, one of the window panes is broken, there is no handle on the door and no heating. I keep my warm jacket on but my feet are starting to go numb with cold.

It turns out there is no heating in the school at all. We walk through a corridor to one of the classrooms, where we're having a meeting with the teachers. They have an exhibition of the students' art on the corridor walls and the bright colours of the pictures contrast with the grimy walls and grey corridors. The meeting involves an assessment tool to see what they consider to be the school's strengths and weaknesses, the opportunities they have and what constraints there are, preventing them from realising these opportunities.

The teachers are very vocal and passionate. They praise their school – their students achieve high standards, their school is an example to others, not just in terms of academic achievement, but also in terms of hygiene and physical infrastructure. But the lack of basic supplies such as books and other teaching aids is chronic in all subjects, not to mention the lack of chairs and tables.

The discussion is of course in Albanian, but Lefter, the engineer from the Fier Field Office, translates for me. Towards the end it gets quite heated and I can tell from the expression on some of the teachers' faces that they're not just animated but forceful and angry. I try to imagine the kind of frustration they must feel, teaching in such horrendous conditions, freezing classrooms, dilapidated walls, no handles on the doors, no pictures or posters or teaching aids of any kind. When I speak to the English teacher afterwards, she clarifies the situation for me.

Other NGOs have come here before, asking questions, what do we need, what would we like to see and so on, but nothing has happened. Also, other schools in the area have been renovated by the Municipality, but not this one. The classroom doors – and she points to the bare wooden doors, with gaps between the door frames and the walls – were donated by parents and made by the students, in their woodwork classes.

Have other NGOs spoken to the teachers? I ask.

No, she admits, but they've been to see the Director.

I begin to feel uneasy about our situation here. What right do we have I think, to come here, make the teachers give up most of their lunch break probably to ask them questions and not be able to give, at least at this stage, a definite offer of any help at all? Do we have the right to raise hopes that we cannot fulfil?

I say to Chris that I feel that we should tell the teachers more about our situation, so that they do not have unrealistic expectations of us. We could tell them that we do not have access to unlimited amounts of money, but have to submit proposals to donors and are entirely dependent on whether they accept these proposals and so decide to give us funding. This is why we have to do background research before compiling proposals, which we then hope will be accepted.

And there are so many schools in need, but that, we would not say – nor the fact that it is not just schools we're trying to fund but houses, roads, water supplies, market places, train stations, hospitals. The needs are so great and our capacity to assist, in the face of that, so puny.

As he passes us in the corridor one of the teachers, a young man holding a few stems of yellow mimosa flowers which are just beginning to bloom, plucks one from the bunch and hands it to me.

The next school we visit is in Patos, a few kilometres outside Fier. We are already involved in work with this school, the first phase is completed and we've been given the go-ahead for the next phase to begin. The walls have been replastered, new toilets have been installed (but are not yet in use, because there is no running water) and new doors put in. These doors are remarkable; their smooth surfaces are beautifully planed and varnished.

The director, Nebi Maska, says that all he has in the school are the walls. There are some desks – simple wooden ones and a few books donated by the Ministry of Education, but that is all. He is a large imposing man who talks with intensity and a deep sense of integrity and commitment. He explains that he goes constantly to the Ministry of Education, speaks to the Director and Inspector of Education to get help for the school.

Everyone in my position has a certain bell he has to ring and if he doesn't ring it, nothing will happen, he says. I ask him, through Ira, who interprets, when the situation of lack of funding had begun. He said it started in 1991 when there were not enough books and by 1997 there were no books or supplies of any kind – nothing at all.

He gestures to me to come over to the window. Outside, there's a rough area of earth and gravel in front of the school. Just beyond that is a rubbish dump – a small hill of bottles, tins, plastic cartons, plastic bags and rusted metal. There used to be grass there, he says, and trees. That's what I would like to see here again, not this mud and rubbish but a grassy area for the children to play in, bordered by trees.

When we arrive at the school, it's break time and the children are playing outside. We pull up in the Land Rover and they crowd around us, some of them even wanting to follow us inside. When we leave, we climb the hill behind the school. Part of the road is a sea of mud and the Land Rover stalls. The driver puts it into four wheel drive and we crawl slowly through the thick mud ruts, away from Patos school, leaving behind the brick building with its garland of rubbish, its gleaming doors and its dream of running water, grass and trees and summer shade.

10

Entila is a young Albanian woman who works at the Business Link School which offers English classes. I'd met her and Brian, the British manager of the school, at Rupert's farewell party. Rupert's wife is Romanian and they are going back to live there. I'd mentioned to Brian that I would be interested in doing some teaching and the next day Entila phoned me and asked me to come along and meet the boss.

It was pitch black when I got there. I could see nothing at all in front of me and I had to grope my way, inch by inch, along the walls. When I heard faint voices I headed in that direction and after rounding a corner there was a tiny glimmer of light. As I got closer I saw it came from two candles burning on the reception desk.

Yes, no power, sighed Entila.

The formalities were minimal, and swift. Brian presided, as the boss spoke little English himself, and after a brief discussion regarding my qualifications and experience, I was offered a contract to teach English on Saturday mornings.

*

Yesterday I managed to lose the mobile phone and the laptop froze on me. Chris said not to worry about the phone.

Since I've worked for IRC he said, I've lost four cars, three motorbikes, three desktops, two laptops and hundreds of dollars.

At first I did not believe him. Someone as careful and conscientious as Chris simply could not have mislaid so many large objects. But he assured me it was true. He was working in Africa at the time and the things were stolen.

One of the stolen cars turned up again, he said. I got a tip off from someone to wait at a crossroads and the car was full of young guys with guns. We stopped them, checked the engine serial number and I said to them – this is my car and they said yes it is – but what do you do?

They had a lot of guns –

I managed to unfreeze the laptop, eventually. Remove the battery, I'd been told. By pushing every conceivable part of the plastic casing, I found a part that moved a little, which meant another part could move. I lifted it up and the screen went blank. It restarted again successfully.

Chris, Whitney, Melinda and I went to eat at the Berlin restaurant. It's near Ravena's, a café-bar with lots of tables outside, which Whitney says is popular in the summer. This is the much-coveted residential area of town known as The Blok, where the dictator, Enver Hoxha, used to live. His residence now houses the government. All the members of the political elite lived within the few streets that formed The Blok, in what we'd now call a gated area, with the additional extra of armed guards. The Berliner Restaurant street – its real name is Rruga Vaso Pasha – is wide and tree-lined and the buildings are either modern or newly renovated. Only the politically 'important' people lived here, with space to park their cars. Other people did not have cars and were not allowed to walk down this street during the communist era.

Whitney is the Field Co-ordinator at Elbasan, a town south-east of Tirana, and she tells me about the other side of the work we do here, that I'd glimpsed at the Naim Frasheri school in Fier. Families who had taken in Kosovar refugees during the crisis in 1999 were known as 'host families'. One of IRC's programmes included the renovation of the houses of these 'host families'. But only some of the houses which had hosted the refugees were renovated. Others were not. And every day, Whitney says, she has people coming to the office or stopping her in the street, wanting her to do something about *their* houses. Some of them are very angry, some shout at her, accuse her of taking bribes, of corruption, and she's even had death threats.

No matter how much we explain to them that we have financial constraints as well, they don't believe me, she said. They're convinced I'm taking bribes as that's the way things work here. But what can I do? I agree it's unfair, I can agree that their houses are sometimes in more need of repair than others we've worked on, but I can't do anything about it. Donika, who is her Field Officer, once became so exasperated with the complaints of a host family that she said to them – Well, no-one *asked* you to take in refugees.

Of course, Whitney said, we shouldn't say that, we're supposed to be polite at all times, but we are human too, we have pressures and limits and constraints as well, and so it just came out.

After the meal, Chris said let's have coffee in the Rogner tomorrow and read *The Sunday Times*. He went home, and Whitney, Melinda and I went to the Piano Bar, further along Rruga Vaso Pasha, to drink more wine. After the sunny day, there was a definite chill in the air, the sky was clear, the stars very bright. A couple of fires were burning by the roadside, as we walked home.

11

Much of Albania's territory has a long history of being overrun, fought over, squabbled over, and parcelled out by other nations. Its boundaries have had a restless quality to them and even since independence in 1912, territory has been taken from Albania as part of the settlement after the Balkan Wars and the two World Wars. The loss of Kosova, which was given to Serbia, was most keenly felt. One person I spoke to, Ali Boja, lives near Elbasan, and took in a family of Kosovar refugees in 1999. When I asked him how he regarded Kosova he accepted that it was a separate country but said that 'in our hearts, we are one people'.

Particularly in the mountainous north, there is a history of family and political life being joined in a clan or tribe based system. The Kanun of Lek Dukagjin was an attempt to formalise law and codes of behaviour in the 15th century, but has become most famous for its rules regarding the blood feud. If a life is taken, the Kanun demands a life in return – but only one, and not necessarily the life of the one who committed the original crime, but any male member of that tribe or clan. To satisfy the honour of the clan, a life is demanded. Set down as a way of containing and limiting violence rather than instigating it, nevertheless, it has led to a series of retributive killings, which means in practical terms, that the male members of many families live lives of virtual incarceration, for to go outside the house is to risk death. While incidents of blood-feud killings virtually disappeared in the decades of the communist regime, they have reappeared again, despite efforts of conciliatory organisations, which work to settle disputes without bloodshed.

Ismail Kadare is Albania's most famous writer. In his novel *Broken April*, he gives a vivid and lyrical account of the feelings and fate of one young man involved in such a feud. The Kanun is described by one of the characters in the story as *like all great things, [it] is beyond good and evil.*

In a conference held in France in 2003 various experts on the Kanun explained its workings to the French senate. The *gjakmarrje* or blood feud nowadays they said, is being used as a cover to enact personal revenge and settle mafia scores. According to Maqo Lakrori, criminal activities are hiding behind so called traditional customs, using the name of the Kanun as a front to serve their own private interests.

Personal vendettas, the settling of old scores, and current rivalry between people involved in criminal activities, are certainly a feature of modern life in Albania. But as explicitly pointed out above, the Kanun Ismail Kadare's character is talking about, is not the one that is operational today.

The mountains certainly have a vivid presence. There is something unearthly about them and I could imagine that living among them would have profound effects. Perhaps these effects include the mixing of the imaginary with the real, which is what Kadare's character experiences, as well as heightening that very Balkan blending of different times so that the past feels like a very close and present companion. But what I was told in the Security Briefing was quite simple. The mountainous northern areas of Albania were lawless and dangerous and I was strongly advised not to go there on my own.

Almost a century earlier the intrepid writer and traveller Edith Durham had spent a lot of time with various tribes-people of the north. With a local guide, she had travelled on horseback through the mountains, enjoying the hospitality of many different clans. Her stories and adventures are recounted in *High Albania*. The tradition of hospitality to the guest in the northern regions was elevated almost to an art form, and was a

different facet of the customs of behaviour codified by
Lek Dukagjin. Albanians I spoke to confirmed this idea
that the guest was seen as a semi-divine being. Kadare's
character in *Broken April* describes the guest as coming
...directly from the realms of destiny or fate.

This is because you do not know what train of events
might follow in the wake of his appearance. The safety
of your guest became your responsibility. If anything
happened to him while you were responsible for him, your
honour became involved in the same way that it would if
something happened to a member of your family. Which is
why the 'knock at the door' brought so many possibilities
along with it, including those of disastrous consequences.
However odd it may appear to Western minds, this was
the way it was. Hospitality was sacred. This attitude
towards hospitality still lingers in Albania today, but the
chaos that has followed from the break-up of the accepted
order of things has brought about an unpredictability in
people's behaviour. Personal scores were being settled and
criminal activities were being undertaken, using the blood
feud as a mask. The mountainous north, traditionally
more accustomed to settling their own affairs rather than
looking to the forces of law and order, was particularly
unpredictable.

12

We are driving to Shkodra, in the north of Albania.
Leaving at seven in the morning, it takes us three hours
to cover the one hundred and twelve kilometres from

Tirana. Because it has not rained for a while, the mud by the roadside has turned to dust. It's a sunny, cloudless day, though the air is chilly in the early morning. Early it may be, but Tirana is already busy. On the outskirts, we pass a butcher's shop, where large chunks of animal body parts are hung on hooks. There is no front door to this shop, it has a short makeshift wooden awning, but otherwise is open to the street. Half hidden by the end of the stall and half on the pavement, a black bull lies on its back, legs in the air, a dark pool around its head. Butcher's shops obviously double as abattoirs here.

We pass pony carts, with one or two people sitting up front, and in the back, sometimes a child, but more often hay or sacks or pieces of wood. We stop in Lezha for coffee. There are hills on either side of the road but after Lezha they become very bare, with lots of whitish stone showing through the scrubby brown growth. Some grazing cows by the side of the road with ropes tied round their horns, are accompanied by their owners. Some are being led from one grazing place to the next. Sometimes you see donkeys standing quite still, eyes closed. They're possibly asleep.

We pass women working in fields, turning over the earth with what look like small spades. Many of the women wear white scarves on their heads. The colour of the earth here is bright, ranging from reddish-orange to mustard. Hay for the animals' feed is stacked round poles, and because it's been eaten from the middle down, the remaining stacks look like long, thin people, sheltered by parasols or umbrellas.

In some places, the road is so full of holes they cannot always be avoided and we are shaken relentlessly from side to side. We see women washing clothes – sometimes at a well, once from a pipe that constantly gushed out water. The road passes very close to the mountain, which is almost all grey stone, with a few thorny, spiky bushes growing out from between stones and rocks. But in the distance, not clear, but hazy, there are much higher mountains, topped with snow.

Shkodra is a fair-sized town that lies in a plain surrounded by mountains. There is a feeling of Asia here, with its wide blue skies and mountain air and leisurely pace of life, as if lots of little villages have clustered into one space. According to Melinda, the Field Officer in Shkodra, the character of the people is different too – they've got a better sense of humour, she claims. Most of Shkodra was levelled in an earthquake in 1979, but there is an old part which escaped and we drive through it. Apart from the old market and bazaar in Kruje, these are the first old buildings I've seen in Albania. Their peeling, pale yellow walls and delicate wrought-iron balconies have a sense of history and time. There's a sleepy feeling to this town, where many of the houses have a small area of ground where trees and vines grow, chickens bob their heads and roosters crow. There are the usual markets, with the streets lined with fruit and vegetable sellers, clothes, bales of cloth and carpets.

In the IRC field office, I sit on the balcony with Ira for a while. On the balcony of the house opposite, a large woman in a blue dress sifts flour into a tub. A child plays in the garden. The woman walks slowly down the steps, says something to the child, goes back up, picks up the large sieve again. I decide she must have a bread-baking business, for the tub is waist-high, and full of flour. The whole scene feels slowed down, as if time is napping here, sprawled in the early afternoon sun. The woman sifts flour, the child plays and a cat jumps from a tree onto a roof. The street is silent and there's not a breath of wind.

Near the town centre is an imposing mosque with a shiny reflective dome, which looks as if it's been covered in silver paper. It throws white light in your eyes, like tinsel. It was a donation from Saudi Arabia, built in 1991. Melinda says she hears the call to prayer every day but has never actually seen anyone go into it. Close by is a statue of four armed men, with determined and visionary looks on their faces, which have broad cheekbones and clearly-defined jaw-lines. I ask Melinda who they are.

Heroes defending Albanian independence, she says. Or the four guys with guns, as we call them.

We go to see the TB clinic and the train station, two projects funded by IRC. Work at the TB clinic has not started yet, as agreement for funding has only just been given by the World Health Organisation. The clinic has a garden and trees at the front, bestowing an atmosphere of calm and rest. So restful in fact that, round the back, the crumpled, rusted shell of an ambulance lies on its side and two stray dogs are stretched out on the gravel, sunning themselves.

Steps and plasterwork are crumbling, but otherwise the hospital looks clean and welcoming. The plan is to build a dispensary and separate the outpatients department from the actual hospital, which is important in this type of clinic to prevent cross-infection. Old garages are also going to be converted into an office, a well is to be dug, new pipe lines laid to ensure an uncontaminated water supply, new doors and windows fitted and new toilets built.

Two trains pass through Shkodra every day. We arrive as the midday train pulls into the station. Only a handful of people get off and even fewer are waiting to get on.

But it was a very different story in the time of the crisis of 1999, when thousands of refugees arrived on these trains, Shkodra being the first stop across the border from Kosova. It was used as a transit centre for refugees and suffered damage as a result. But the worst damage was done in 1997, Melinda said, when it was trashed during the riots – windows and doors were destroyed and the restaurant became unusable.

The first phase of rehabilitation is now under way – the leaking roof is being repaired, as are doors, windows, electrical wiring and toilets. In the second phase, replastering and paintwork will be done, as well as the filling in of large gaps in walls, caused by subsidence. Melinda also hopes that there will be enough money to include some basic furniture – seats or wooden benches, so that people using the station in the future will have somewhere to sit down. At the moment, there are only two dilapidated benches in the upstairs waiting area. We drive back to the IRC offices, passing the statue of the four heroes with their eyes fixed resolutely on the distant mountains and the glittering dome of the empty mosque.

The Via Egnatia and the Other Reality

Albania is a land bristling with mountains
Dora d'Istria

1

The power goes out in the office and the phone is completely dead. I speak to Genc who comes to have a look at it, lifts the receiver, pushes buttons, checks the connections and shrugs his shoulders. It may be that someone is using it, he says, making some illegal connection. Who can say? Maybe it will work again later. We'll see.

I ask him if phones are tapped here, explaining this is common practice in the UK. Oh no, he says, who would bother. Then we get onto the subject of having to pay an extra 'duty' on things. Computers have to be ordered from abroad and so take some time to be shipped in. And then, Genc says, you may have to pay extra for them to be released. You shouldn't have to pay more, but that's what happens. It happened to me, when I was coming into the country with four bags. I had to pay at the airport before they would give me the bags.

I asked him where he had been. It turned out he'd been studying for his PhD at Iowa University. Genc always wears a scarf round his neck and has a slightly wistful, almost dreamy expression. He's quiet, does not smile much and looks rather sad most of the time, as if he doesn't want to be here. He looks out of the window or to one side of you, when he talks.

At lunch time it pours with rain and there are flashes of lightning in the sky and thunder right overhead. I love the drama of this weather. And when I leave work all the little roads are awash with puddles and the water pipe road is practically impassable and there are now two pipes spouting water instead of just one but for some reason I feel very happy, avoiding all these puddles in the dark.

2

Ina works at the Business Link School, along with Entila, and is also a student, studying humanities. She says she only recently came back to Tirana. She left ten years ago with her parents and has been living in Corfu since then. She takes me from Rruga Kavaje to the FEFED Bank, where I'm teaching my English class. Tirana didn't used to be like this she says, it used to be clean and tidy, not with all this rubbish lying everywhere, muddy streets and broken pavements. And there were very few cars.

A soldier with a Kalashnikov stands outside the FEFED bank. When I leave the building, after teaching my class, the soldier twitches his gun automatically into alert. Along the wide boulevard outside the Rogner Hotel there are people selling cigarettes, sweets, black seeds and roasted chestnuts. Small fires smouldering in tin trays are covered with a wire grille and the chestnuts sit on the grille, roasting slowly.

I walk up to Scanderbeg Square and have a coffee at the Piazza café which is tucked behind the museum, with its imposing and rather beautiful mosaic of striding and purposeful workers. The piazza café feels like an oasis, its large tables have sheltering umbrellas and are arranged around a fountain. The air is crisp and clear and the light is so fresh, pervasive and direct, that I feel as if something I've been starved of all my life, without knowing what it was, is carried in this light. After the coffee I walk up the Rruga Durresit, coming out at a small side road I'd walked along the day before with Xhina, one of my colleagues. The road goes past a very ancient and dilapidated building, with a balcony and peeling plaster and a palm tree in front of it.

Modern Albanian buildings are neither picturesque nor durable. While there are some old buildings – Xhina assures me of this – the cracked, colonial-looking one with its elegantly thin iron railings, skewed balconies and ruined exterior being one of them – the majority of buildings are modern. A few of them affect some kind of style – painted exteriors with bright colours. Most are concrete apartment blocks, stained and dilapidated, reflecting I feel, the grim reality of communist life, with its emphasis on joyless functionality.

School buildings look like prisons from the outside, concrete blocks erected quickly and cheaply. Some of the ones we visited were built in the mid-1980s, we were told. Less than two decades later, the stairs inside are broken, the plaster is crumbling, the doors, if there are any, hanging off and some of the classrooms are locked up because they're in such a bad state that they're unusable.

3

Dust in my eyes going up Rruga Abdyl Frasheri to the FEFAD bank. The stinging eyes scenario. The bike stall that I'd noticed last weekend is there again. It's on the corner as I come round from the old stadium, tucked behind a scaffolding covered with bright corrugated tin. The stall consists of an upturned bike, and attached to it somehow is this grimy old ex-café umbrella with ice-cream written in enticing faded lettering on it. Grey inner tubes dangle from the inside of the parasol.

When I reach the FEFAD bank the soldier on guard outside swings his rifle and smiles slightly at me. I'm a familiar face now. The door isn't open yet but Mirita soon arrives and says Luis is just coming with the key. Luis arrives wearing a very stylish black coat, sprints up the steps and unlocks the door. I don't believe we've met he says, I'm Luis – and he shakes my hand. His English is excellent and his accent sounds more German than Albanian. After he lets us in he then says he has to go back to change and shave. No need I say. He has a slight designer stubble. Off whisks Luis in his mustard Mercedes and Mirita and I climb one flight and I go into the kitchen to fix some coffee. Then I realise I've forgotten the photocopies for the class and by the time the coffee is made and I've chatted to Brian who arrives just after me, and made more photocopies, it's well after 10.15 and last week I told the class to try to be punctual and what kind of example is this I'm setting?

Someone is drilling just outside the window of the room Brian's supposed to be teaching in and he suggests we put the two classes together in my room as there is only a total of six students. I offer to take the class. We end up having a heated debate about cultural differences and all the students interrupt each other. Would you say Albanians are people who show their emotions quite readily? I ask. They all say yes.

Outside the window of the room where I teach there's a building with peeling walls and cracked façades, and there are clothes hung out on the balconies. There's a different soldier standing outside when I leave, the usual Kalashnikov hanging from his shoulder. He stares at me and I smile at him. I think to myself that at least it's his job to look at people, but all the others who stare as I walk down the street, hardly have that excuse.

After teaching my English class I find a secluded café table near the Blu Bar, where I can write. It backs onto a little grove of trees with a low wall and railing separating it from the grassy triangular park that forms the corner between the wide boulevard that goes up past the Rogner Hotel and the Pyramid – and Abdyl Frasheri, my home stretch. It's warm today, it's spring, people are out walking in the sunshine and the scent of the yellow mimosa flowers is sometimes even stronger than the petrol fumes.

A man in a dusty jacket is lying stretched out on the grass, seemingly asleep. A couple of young men go past, they stop, one of them flicks the man's kerchief across his cheek, but he doesn't stir.

I feel optimistic today – if I understand 'spirit' as anything, it's that uplifting feeling of expansion that transfigures everything around you because *you* feel different. It is akin to being filled with warm light and the sensation is of joy that rises up until there isn't room for anything that could disturb or interfere with that.

It's a feeling that bridges gaps and separations, that

makes complete, that joins and takes flight. It connects you to a much bigger world. It's really the pursuit of that feeling that I'm after. The search is always on, no matter what the backdrop, the changing landscape or scenery.

The only flowering thing I've seen here so far is a yellow mass of mimosa. They burn like brilliant fiery bushes in the large gardens of the consulates and the government buildings. These gardens are always protected by soldiers, who stand or shuffle a little, holding Kalashnikovs slung over their shoulders.

In the communist era, there were certain streets people were not allowed to walk down. It doesn't seem to be so very different now as far as I can see, with various areas cordoned off, soldiers with guns standing behind the yellow tape.

While most people are friendly – the woman in the Pinocchio café, the woman who has the kiosk by the bridge, where I buy *byrek*, the man with the bookshop where I've bought postcards – some have an offhand, almost sullen attitude. There's a deep sense of suspicion that is tangible, it's in the air, and there is also resentment – for example, the tremendous frustration that was voiced at the Naim Frasheri school. Brian talks about the Director of one of the English schools who has the old communist way of thinking. If anyone disagrees with him, whether it's a teacher or his secretarial staff, he sacks them. He's sacked several people in the past few months, Brian says. He *has* to have total control. He cannot be in the wrong – he justifies everything he does. That kind of iron-tight thinking hardly makes for flexibility and tolerance of differences, but he has always lived his life under a regime of profound conventionality – to what others have decided the rules should be. You adapt and adopt a similar rigidity in your own thinking.

But to understand the roots of this suspicion, resentment and frustration, one need only consider the history of Albania, particularly the most recent events. The Albanian people have almost *always* had to fight – sometimes successfully, other times not – against successive foreign domination – the Roman, Venetian and then the Ottoman Empire. Their initial euphoria at the success, after world War II, of Enver Hoxha and his communist partisans, was quickly followed by disillusion, as his government turned out to be the most controlling and oppressive of them all. Now, less overt, but still there, is the mafia. How do you arrive at a place where you deal openly with people? Albanians are mostly warm, friendly and hospitable, but with a long history of repression. Perhaps because of this inheritance of control, breeding secrets, fear and suspicion, there is this slumbering anger, resentment and frustration. Entila works long hours at the English School for very little pay and puts up with treatment no Western employee would tolerate, but Brian has said to her to stick it out for a month longer, until her contract ends. The problem of course is that people are afraid of losing even their miserable, badly paid jobs.

Perhaps because they have so few real flowers, Albanians show a great fondness for artificial ones. They are all over my apartment, these slightly slimy-feeling cloth monstrosities. There are whole stalls that sell only them – as well as delightful plastic plant pots.

Some things just break your heart – an old woman in lumpy clothes, a shapeless old skirt, leaning over a stall, with the usual modest selection of cigarettes and chocolate bars. An old man sitting on a bench by the puddles bordering the Rruga Comuna Parisit, near my apartment, with a neon pink radio in his hands, fiddling with knobs, a look of puzzled concentration on his face. Inside the old stadium people are playing football. Outside the locked gates, an old man stands, his hands behind his back, his fingers moving in rhythm over a string of beads, covered in bright yellow plastic.

4

George came into my office the other day, with a pen and piece of paper in his hand, asking if I'd like to come on a trip he's organising, up Dajti mountain.

We're all going to jump off a cliff he says. Lemming-like, I sign up with enthusiasm.

So on Saturday morning, in a three car convoy, we head out of town for the big mountain that lies just behind Tirana. On the way, we pass an imposing building fronted with carved statues. It's in a terrible state of dilapidation, but we wonder what it might have been, we're curious about its history, who might once have lived here, how it managed to escape being demolished.

The narrow road winds uphill, with sharp corners, gravelly verges, fewer potholes than in the city, and steep drops. Eventually we turn off at a gravel track which peters out into grass and mud. We stop when we can't go any further. Ahead of us are sandy rocks. We climb round and up, over rocks and through green bushes, until we come to the top of a small cliff. George then gives us all a lecture on how to put on the harness for abseiling. When someone starts talking and is clearly not paying attention, he reminds us that our life could depend on putting the harness on properly. Suitably subdued, we listen in silence. One by one we attach the harness and go off the side of the cliff, which was not very high, and the sand tended to stick on the rope, making it difficult to pay through the metal carabiner. So movement was fairly slow. I was just beginning to get the hang of it, when I was at the bottom.

We then drive up to the top of the mountain, and have lunch at the restaurant there, with a superb view of the valley. From a distance, where its broken, muddy and litter-strewn streets cannot be seen, Tirana looks like any other town. Beyond it is the distant blue horizon of the Adriatic Sea. And in the other direction, there's the last flank of mountain, pasted with a film of slender trees with bunches of snow around their roots.

On the descent, there are children by the roadside, clutching yellow mimosa blossoms, the first colour to emerge out of the greys and browns and dark greens of the pine trees. We stop and buy some. I have some now, in a vase in the flat and their perfume is thick and heavy and their initial sweetness has an underlying bitterness, a sharpness, an acrid tang.

5

There is something about travelling along a truly ancient route that links you both to the land itself and to human history, in a very immediate way. Of course this would be more true if one was walking and placing one's feet on the earth itself, but there is still a sense of entering history, moving into a different time, a different present, in the knowledge that people have travelled this way for centuries, with all their hopes fears and purposes, carrying their lives and their merchandise, in an age when travel was necessarily slow, giving you plenty of time for contemplation. The road from Durres on Albania's west coast, to the town of Elbasan close to Albania's eastern border, follows the Via Egnatia, an old trade route from Roman times that continues on to Ohrid in Macedonia, then through Greece and Turkey to Istanbul.

Elbasan lies in a plain, surrounded by mountains. On one side of the plain is the town itself and on the other – occupying an area which at first sight is just as extensive – is a grotesque array of rusted metal pipes and tubes. This skeletal arrangement is the remains of a metallurgical factory, built by the Chinese during the communist regime. A trail of yellowish smoke drifts from a chimney and settles in the air over the town.

The road from Tirana to Elbasan runs along the mountain tops, giving views over layers of peaks becoming fainter and mistier with distance. When it begins its descent into the valley, curling and looping back on itself, one side of the road is built up like an embankment. Parts of it erupt into mosaics of determined and heroic workers, grasping their hammers and welding instruments, staring past you, out across the Elbasan valley and the sickly yellow smoke dribbling from the chimney.

The morning is grey and overcast. Just past the outskirts of Tirana, we cross a bridge that was closed for a long time because parts of it caved in or fell away. Whitney told me that it had partially collapsed because some excavation work had undermined the bridge's foundations. Capsized dumper trucks and tractors lie in the river like forlorn dinky toys. In the communist era when very few people had cars, the only vehicles using this road were the big Chinese trucks, transporting materials to and from the vast factory complex. But we might still have been in this time, or in any time during the past hundreds of years, for the road is empty of vehicles.

As we climb up the winding mountain road, heading for Elbasan, we leave behind all signs of habitation and are surrounded by the wildness of the mountains. The landscape becomes stark and bare, a sea of brown-peaked frozen waves, breathtakingly beautiful. Clearly, we are in another world, one that belongs to nature.

We had left Tirana at 7.30 in the morning, which meant getting up an hour earlier than usual, and I was finding it difficult to wake up. But Chris is his usual cheerful self, eager to talk, asking questions. What poetry do you read? Do you believe in astrology? Do you believe in God?

We need to talk about this in a café, with good coffee and plenty of time I say. My mind is fuzzed and blank, it's not responding, it has twined itself lovingly with the thin cloud that dances on the mountain-peaks, throwing off a snow as light as the reflection of emotion in water.

But Arif answers Chris's last question and describes his understanding of God as an energy that inhabits everything, is present in everything that is, though we are not always able to perceive it. I like Arif's description. Chris wrinkles his brow and thinks about it. He claims not to believe in God but I wonder if it's a certain definition of God that he rejects.

It begins to snow a little, small flurries of white blurring the sky with the landscape. The road curls along the top of one of the mountains, with valleys falling away on either side. Some of the peaks are rocky, slanted and so thin they look almost shaved to a point, like giant pencils.

By the time we get to Elbasan the sky is still grey and a light rain is falling. We are here to take part in the opening ceremony of the covered marketplace whose construction we have funded. But before going to the marketplace we visit Kuqan school, whose renovation we are also funding. There are the usual broken steps, plywood doors, dust and grime in the classrooms, shabby, rickety desks. The classrooms are unheated apart from the nursery, where there is a wood-burning stove, which fails to make much impact on the whole room, but does take the worst chill off the air. The little ones are not free to move around, but sit at low tables, crowded together. They all gaze at us fixedly as we talk to their teacher. This open and unembarrassed curiosity is also present in the older students in the other classrooms. They stand up politely when we come in. And do the same when we leave, with an enthusiastic chorus of *mirupafshim* (goodbye).

The upstairs of this school is blocked off because it's unusable. The rooms there have no doors and the tiles are completely broken up. There are window frames but no windows. In one room, there are piles of excrement on the floor. But outside, there are neat whitewashed houses, with little yards where vines are threaded up sticks and across a lattice of wire at the top, so that in summer their leaves will provide shade. In a nearby hay barn an old woman is pulling out hay with a long fork. And in front of the school, rows of young saplings have recently been planted. In a few years time they will transform the bare brown earth, and provide shade for the children.

We then head for the marketplace. We stand around in the damp and chill for about half an hour waiting for the mayor, as the ceremony cannot begin until he arrives. I wonder if his delay is calculated to emphasise his importance, or if he simply has a disregard for time. Whitney has mentioned that she has had some difficult dealings with the mayor. His actual involvement in the construction of the covered marketplace has been minimal, but his consent has been necessary at every step of the negotiations. At times, Whitney has hinted, he has been obstructive, deliberately delaying the procedure, just to show his importance, and to show that he is in control. But despite all the difficulties, the project has been completed. The fruit and vegetable vendors, who have previously had to sell their wares out in the open, in the chill and wet of winter as well as the baking heat of summer, will soon have a covered area to protect them from the elements. So Whitney is quietly triumphant, and tolerates the mayor's impoliteness, or deliberate show of power, whichever it might be, with patience and a brisk but professional manner.

The mayor, when he finally arrives, turns out to be a large man with a loud voice. He gives a speech in which, according to Whitney's whispered translation, he takes most of the credit for the undertaking, as if it had been his idea and had enjoyed his unflagging commitment. Whitney's speech is brief, praising all involved and not forgetting to give due thanks to the mayor. She cuts the red ribbon, marking the official opening and then things move very quickly. The vendors are inside and have set up shop with amazing speed. Within minutes the counters are piled with scales and vivid colours – apples, oranges, lettuces, leeks, red and green peppers. Customers throng the aisles and the metal roof resounds with chatter. Chris and I stockpile fruit and vegetables from one of the nearest vendors and we pile them in the car.

After the ceremony we visit another school, driving on the Librazhd to Kukës road. Librazhd is small but has an elegant curving main street, lined with trees. On the way there we pass an old woman in black, with a white scarf round her head, digging gravel and sand to make mortar. On the brown mountainsides, there are trees with white and pink blossom. At the Hotolishti school, which we are proposing to fund, some rooms are full of rubbish, as if it had been bombed. The floorboards are wet and we are told that if it rains, the ceilings leak so badly that the rooms are closed and classes abandoned. To get to the playground you have to climb up a long flight of steps. There is a fine view from the top, but it is dangerous for there are no protective barriers.

On the way back, Gramoz, our driver, stops and buys some purple flowers. The clouds have gone, the sun is out. Some of the peaks, still capped with snow, are dazzling in this light. We seem to be higher up than everything that's visible.

In Tirana, the evening sunlight catches pieces of buildings, clutches at them, in some rosy sense of memory – walls turn deep and mysterious, puddles become wells of gold and the few soft, green-feathered branches of drifting trees, shine in the evening glow. We drive slowly through the narrow back lanes, swaying up and down with each pothole.

In the twilight, when I walk down the steps from the office, a rat saunters across the path below. Mattresses, chairs, boots, tiles, and pieces of wood are piled up in the river.

An old woman, bent over from a huge sack piled on her back, rummages through the litter bin. The water from the broken pipe has filled the hole in the street and overflowed into the road. Two boys float toy boats tied to string on the murky lake that the road has turned into. In the rooster street with the thin strip of muddy, rubbish-clogged yard where the hens and roosters peck, a scrawny tree has burst into white blossom, a sudden spillage of emotion, a rustle of light against the flaky grey grime of the buildings.

I come home with a bunch of flowers given to me at the Elbasan market opening ceremony. The flowers are vivid shades of yellow and orange.

6

I turn up as usual for my Saturday English class but I am told when I got there that it has been cancelled. No reason is given. So I take the chance to visit the Art Gallery and the Museum. Many of the pictures in the Art Gallery are painted in the Socialist Realist style. They do not have that exaggerated visionary look about them, the glorification of the workers that you find in the Russian communist school. In one picture several people are walking through a mountain pass, in deep snow. In another, entitled *The Partisan*, a young man is reading. He looks as though he is outside by a camp-fire, for there is a deep yellow glow around his face and chest. But that might have been symbolic. One painting in a naïve tradition, similar to Rousseau, shows several young women on the porch outside a house in the country. There are one or two showing workers doing 'good work'. One, which I find disturbing, shows a family scene.

Both the room and table are bare, and though the people are all sitting at the table except for one who is by the stove, the way they are arranged and the expressions on their faces gives a Hopper type of alienation to the whole scene – a family maybe, but they all have their private worlds and agendas which show in the positioning of their limbs and faces, turned away from each other.

Then there is a whole room of sculpted heads – there's a Hoxha head, with that slightly contemptuous expression you find on the faces of dictators. Others are beautiful, some are deliberately distorted, a few are of old people with lined faces, some of the faces are smooth, with plaited hair, one or two with oriental eyes.

The Museum has many archaeological finds on display as well as historical maps, but what is most striking is the whole floor dedicated to those who were killed during the communist regime. Rows upon rows of names, all listed in alphabetical order, with flowers (artificial of course) placed at regular intervals on the floor, as a tribute. Further on there are photographs of various people – party members and dissidents, as well as graphic explanations of torture devices which I thankfully cannot understand, it all being in Albanian. There is also a display of the instruments of torture and a little room representing the cell in which prisoners were kept. Sharp metal objects dangle from the walls, which are splashed with blood – mock blood I presume. I look inside the open door but I don't go in.

Outside the Museum, Scanderbeg Square is drenched in sunlight. I meet Chris and we go for coffee, making our way through the warren of kiosks and café tables that line the side of the boulevard.

Do you want to learn Albanian? Chris asks. He's always asking questions. Do you want to stay here, do you regret being married, how long were you married? Do you want to sit in the sun or shade? And I say a mixture, and we find a table with dappled sunlight falling over it, exactly right, and we talk of political systems and the dictatorships and wars of the last century and what it means for humanity and what the future may become and he says he doesn't want to become like many of the people who do this kind of work, at home nowhere really, relating to their friends via a computer screen.

And the sun is warm but not hot and there is no flicker of movement in the still air. It's so quiet and peaceful that it's hard to believe we're almost in the city centre. There is no loud music playing and no people passing. There is the possibility of intimacy here and it's intimacy I realise, that I need, to feel a close connection, no matter where I am. Sitting in this quiet café garden in dappled sunlight, talking to someone about the things that matter to me, I realise that it is intimacy that gives me a feeling of belonging. At the same time as it deftly removes you from time and place, it pours you into it as well, so that a part of you remains there, just as you carry away with you the dust and the light and the scents that have filtered into your bloodstream. This gives energy to the other reality you step back into when you leave the place – the dust and broken flagstones, the heaped rubbish, the gaping manholes. This was a glimpse of something that feeds the soul and lets a sense of gratitude rise up into the sunlight.

7

A gypsy woman with a child in her arms tugged at my sleeve the other day and wouldn't give up. I like the way the gypsy women dress, with their long colourful skirts, their bands of woven cloth around their heads. They spot you in a crowd and train their children too, to come after you and persist. Sometimes I do give them a coin, sometimes I hold out, from stubbornness. Really, I'd rather give to the man with one leg who sits on the bridge, or the old woman with tiny legs that are set askew to her body. She always sits on a little box, near the church on the Rruga Kavaje – tiny as a child, scarf round her head. One day I gave her 50 lek and she cried out – I don't know if it was in delight or disgust.

Chris told me that he had once handed some coins to an old woman whose back was bent over and she was walking slowly and with obvious difficulty, along the street. She unleashed a stream of Albanian at him, and was clearly annoyed. Sometimes it's hard to figure out. Some people beg for money, others sit on the bare pavements, or on a piece of cardboard with a few coins in front of them, and still others have their fierce pride and feel deeply insulted if you offer them money.

The scrawny trees in the strips of muddy yard tucked behind the main street, are turning white, with a pale green flash of leaves. However shabby the streets may be, the sunlight is striking, direct, hard-hitting. Light that you can feel, light that cuts and slices. An absence of wind and a light that tunnels into you, wakes you like a hand pressed on your arm. The sun warms my hands as I pick my way among the puddles and the ruts of mud in the side streets. There's the man with the grey hair and the cap who sells cigarettes near the bridge. There's the young girl with the round cheeks and enormous eyes I buy a baguette from, and the woman who has the *byrek* kiosk who smiles and speaks English to me. Ilya, who asks me about idioms, Gramoz, who smiles shyly, Eva, who gives me extra helpings of soup and winks at me, Olga who takes my arm as we walk along the street, Chris, who quotes Goethe, Ionesco and Eliot to me, who picks up my scarf and coils it round his neck.

Frisch weht der Wind der Heimat zu he says and I continue with him.

Mein Irish Kind, wo weilest du?

And we stand on the balcony, look out over the rooftops of Tirana to the comforting silhouette of Dajti mountain in the background, settled like a sunken, angular, dumb and sightless prayer. An inscrutable flag. A hoard of history, where dreams fiddle with the slightest wind, inebriating reality into becoming something we long for, even as we catch its bright scent in the morning's glitter of snow on Dajti's peak.

Life lived in the hectic moment, in the feverish atmosphere of displacement, feels slightly askew. If there really is a path and there really is a place where we feel at home and truly belong, where is this place I've come to? It feels like nowhere on earth, it feels as if I've followed the map to the end of the world and fallen off. It's another geographical order altogether, a place the psyche has strayed into, stumbled on a different plot. I arrived in some scene, where the beginning and end of the drama are not clear to me. The actors have accommodated me quite cheerfully but I do not really know this storyline at all. The rest of the world has vanished, absorbed in its own concerns.

We bring our own designs, our spades, trowels, our big ideas and our bricks and mortar, patch up pipe lines and roads and houses and schools and railway stations, make speeches, accept flowers, drive around in Land Cruisers and hold farewell parties, vanishing as fast as the snow on Dajti mountain. We live in a kind of transit lounge, keeping busy till our flight is called. But it won't be called until I book it. I'm not even sure I can remember where it was I had in mind to go, or so I say. Perhaps I'm afraid to admit to myself what I want, in case it turns out to be another cul-de-sac, another transit lounge. There's a kind of security in renouncing the big ideals, a kind of comfort in the dailyness of things, the small, but tangible, successes.

Frisch weht der Wind – only it doesn't, there is no wind here. *Wo weilest du?* The mountains are ranged behind me and the sea won't let me cross. We're going nowhere. Not yet anyway. I need more time. I'm not ready to move on again. I'm waiting for spring to take hold of the earth and me and shoot desire through me like sap and change and flight and longing. Not for the past, but for the future.

Wo weilest du?

*

It happened a few weeks after I arrived. I was walking through the streets one day when I realised that the sheen of light that my perceptions had been brushed with, had gone. The ability simply to be fascinated and to accept without judgement, had vanished. Most days, though still cold, were clear, the sky a flawless blue, the light connecting you to another perception, becoming a necessary part of you, as penetrating as an emotion. This particular day was overcast, the light felt like grime on my skin, blocking the pores of this new perception. The mud, the potholes, the broken pavements and the grey stained shabbiness of buildings oppressed me. I longed for beautiful architecture, buildings drenched in time and history, celebrating some ideal, whether of grandeur, harmony or beauty, radiating confidence in its construction. Nothing I saw around me responded to this longing. The only colours were the mud-brown of the streets, the grey sludge of the river, the grey of concrete buildings, a few with peeling yellowish plaster. Almost all the people were dressed in black. I felt desolation, poverty and a lack of hope, in my surroundings. A dispirited weariness and a lack of care. Rubbish piled up in the river and in the streets.

I walked on, looking mainly at my feet, because it was necessary to look where you were stepping. There were uncovered manholes, broken paving stones, mud and piled garbage.

I had a contract for three months. I was about half way through it. I thought about how much I'd wanted to go somewhere different, do something I had not done before. This city was my life now. These grey concrete buildings, the ugliness squalor and dirt, the intrinsic lack of anything inspiring or uplifting or remotely beautiful – these were my surroundings, this was what I had chosen, for my life. I crossed one of the bridges overlooking the river. An old mattress, half submerged. Plastic bottles bobbed on its surface and rubbish lined the sides. I made a decision, looking at the brownish-grey water, filled with garbage. I would love this place, despite its ugliness, its rubbish, its unkempt, broken, dilapidated appearance. I was here and I was going to stay here for the immediate future and I was going to love it, too.

I walked on along the streets, looking quite deliberately at everything my eyes fell on and seeing it as something fascinating and loveable in itself, rather than ugly and dispiriting, as I had before.

My feelings of despondency, of wanting my surroundings to be other than what they were and of wanting something from the buildings and the streets, that they clearly could not give me, did not return. What happened instead, was that spring began, very gradually at first, to make itself felt. Then it gathered momentum. The city underwent a transformation. It peeled open as if it had been holding something inside itself, something secret and covered up. It turned into something beautiful.

8

Jean-Paul speaks very rapidly in French and I can hardly understand anything he says. His accent is just the same in English so his English is only marginally more comprehensible to me than his French. He has a kind of flashing see me hear me here-I-am energy that reminds me of Belisha beacons and zebra crossings, like a major warning or alert signal. He tells jokes which I can't understand and don't get. He has a French contempt of not doing things the right way when it comes to food and drink. Chocolate sprinkled on cappuccino is *de rigeur* but when I once put nutella in my coffee, that was too horrifying for him. Though Chris speaks French better than I do and he understands most of what Jean-Paul says, Jean-Paul ridicules him.

You say you speak French but you can't understand *that*?

Jean-Paul makes deliberately provocative statements, designed to get people riled up.

La poésie? C'est vomir les expériences, he says.

I say I disagree with him but I am not sufficiently antagonistic to satisfy his search for prey, so he then reverts to a favourite topic of his, the superiority of the French language over English.

Si on dit tu es belle, he says, listen to the sound of it, it remains with you, it goes to the person and it stays with you as well but if you say 'you are beautiful', it cuts off, sharp, and it does not reach the person.

We are celebrating Charlie's birthday by having a meal at Antonella's. Jean-Paul mixes whiskey with the wine. He is a bit *mephisto* Olga says. We drink *raki* and then go dancing at the Sao Paolo club just up the road from my apartment, we dance and dance, Entila, Blaerta, Cara, Anxhela and I, and Jean-Paul drifts in among us, moving from one to another, very physical, like a boar or a lion or some mixture of wolf and bear, a growling, laughing, rattlesnake of a bear.

*

Melinda invites me to go with her to Kruje. She is on the hunt for a carpet. The sky is a vivid blue, the air crisp and fresh. The sunlight holds that kind of tantalising promise that you can only feel when spring has not yet arrived, but you know that it is on its way and it will come soon, soon. The trees are still bare, but their branches are basking in the sunlight, bleached and silvery. We walk up the cobbled street of the bazaar in Kruje, the dazzling blue of the sky above us and the bright colours of bags and carpets hanging outside the shop fronts.

First we visit the Ethnology Museum. We go through a thick wooden entrance door into a darkened interior. The wooden floorboards and furniture, all the hangings and draperies have been well-preserved and clearly given loving attention. The upstairs rooms are reached by climbing wooden steps. There are low divans, covered with woven rugs. The walls are hung with tapestries. The floorboards creak as we walk over them.

I wander out into the garden, where there is an old well, complete with its own little red tiled roof. There's a view out across the valley, hazy with sunlight. And just below the garden there are more old stone houses with red-tiled roofs. Roosters are crowing. Silence sweeps in, low-winged, and settles on my shoulder.

We go back to the bazaar. In one of the shops, two women are sitting at upright looms, weaving carpets. A pile of them, already woven, lie on the floor. The carpet seller explains that there are three kinds of designs on the woven kilims – floral, geometric and symbolic animal shapes. These designs here, he gestures – are symbolic of the double-headed eagle of Albania. The red and black colours are traditional for Kruje.

Melinda picks a green and blue floral design. I choose one in red and black and undyed white, a symbolic eagle spanning its surface, declaring its kinship both with the azure sky and the dark rock of the mountain peaks.

9

I move into a new apartment, sharing with George and Anna. It's also used by Al and Simon who are based at the Field Office in Shkodra, but like to come to Tirana at weekends. Al is from Australia, and Simon is from Cornwall, England. The apartment is on the eighth floor of a nine floor building in the Rruga Abdyl Frasheri, above the Irish pub and the Fitness Centre. It has a wide balcony which gives you a view out over the city and across to Dajti mountain.

After the move I meet up with Chris, Charlie, Olga and Jean-Paul in the Irish pub. Jean-Paul, in his usual way of trying to provoke a reaction, flicks a little beer in my face. I take his hair (which is long enough to do this) and wipe my face with it, slowly and thoroughly. Charlie is in charge of the Water and Sanitation projects, originally from the English Midlands, but has worked for many years in various parts of the world. He dislikes any kind of emotional confrontation and tends to laugh at any comments or behaviour that could threaten harmony and light-heartedness. He laughs now and asks me, are you trying to seduce Jean-Paul? No, I say. I'm just wiping the beer off my face. I quite enjoy Jean-Paul's deliberately confrontational statements and actions, because I feel that behind his aggressive behaviour, he is trying to make contact. But I think too, that if I was Olga, living with it every day, I would soon tire of the game-playing and long to pull the mask off his face.

The next day Simon and I went for a walk in Tirana Park. We headed there along the road just opposite the apartment, which goes past the Italian supermarket. It took us about ten minutes to reach the park entrance. There were several paths heading up through the woods and the one we chose led past a modern amphitheatre, copied from the Roman pattern. We returned to the main path which followed the curve of the lake, with a grassy area, lightly dotted with trees, between it and the water. A few people dressed in black were sitting there, while their goats and cows grazed. The trees came to an end on the other side of the lake and the path wound through patches of grass and stony wasteland. We ended up in the zoo, a miserable and desolate place. A few lions and tigers paced in cramped, smelly cages. A solitary llama had a little more space and pulled at some dark brown hay, ignoring us. We were told however, that there are plans for improvement, and an open area is being prepared for the big cats.

Afterwards Simon made a confession.

This sounds a bit sissy he said, but I write poetry sometimes. He has spent years managing fitness centres and working as a bouncer and he's into body building and likes to go and sit on his own by the lake and write poetry.

That evening, looking down onto Abdyl Frasheri from the eighth floor, there was thunder in the sky, rain falling on the balcony, car horns, revving engines, and shiny wet headlights. Night city, with the sound of rain falling on tin roofs and the lights sliding by.

As the weather gets warmer – warm enough to walk around in just a T shirt – the feeling of sunlight on my skin returns sensuality to my life. Like the trees we begin to feel that this is surely who we really are, this rising sap, this exuberant new growth.

10

We were going up to Jean-Paul and Olga's apartment. The others had gone on ahead, in another elevator. It was just me and Jean-Paul. His hair had that ranging, wild, determined look about it. He'd had a lot to drink. I never know what to say to Jean-Paul, because he has to begin a conversation and if you start it, he'll either disagree with you or change the subject. He revels in having an audience. And like most performers, he has a longing for a part that does not demand so much of him, that can be quiet and simple and unobserved.

But as soon as there are other people there, he cannot resist – he has to entertain, speak louder than anyone else. Pin someone down with a provocative statement, push them into a reaction.

But the evening has gone on too long and the wine has had its effect. Jean-Paul is no longer ready to jump in to attack. When we went dancing, he would take my arm and put it round his shoulder. Or come up close to me, take my hands in his version of an Albanian dance, mixed with a kind of tango and an African voluptuousness. And his hair would fall over his eyes and he would push his face close to me.

We are close together in the lift, because it is very small. He leans against the back.

You don't like me, he says.

No that's not true, I say. And I think to myself, I just don't know what to say to you. But I do not say this out loud.

I break everything, he says. He's talking quietly, he's drunk and tired.

I destroy everything, that's what I do.

And I see now why he turns life into theatre, wearing his challenging, provocative mask. Underneath it, there is something wounded, that he wants to hide and sometimes, more than anything, wants to reveal.

Once we're all upstairs and sitting down, he launches into a monologue which has different effects on all of us.

Look at us, he says. Look at what we do here. We're all well-paid and what do we do? What do I do? I turn up late to work, I have a meeting with some people, I go for lunch then I leave early and go home. None of us gives a fuck about Albania. We're all full of self-interest. I think only of myself.

We are silent.

Why does the truth make you all so quiet, so *sairyus*? And if there was an emergency here, what would happen? We'd be evacuated. We'd be out of here. We would not have to worry, we'd be safe. What I'd like to see – just sometimes – just *once* – is a little humility.

Olga protests, Charlie just laughs, Chris starts to say something, but Jean-Paul won't allow for any other possible point of view. I say nothing. He has a point – some of the ex-pats are arrogant in a way I find difficult either to accept or ignore. But I'm more interested in his own perception, than his assumption that everyone's motives and feelings are the same as his. I'm more interested in his own self-dislike, that he invoked in the elevator.

I break things, I always break things.

Afterwards, as we walk home, Chris says what Jean-Paul refused to let him say. It's not true. He was talking about himself, but it isn't true that everyone is here purely from self-interest.

Chris is very idealistic and has a passion to help others.

Whoever he talks to feels intrinsically special, in the light of his attention. He quotes poetry as if it was a cloak to cover mud, debris and rubbish, like a veneer of velvet, a flowering moss over concrete and garbage and neglect. He takes flight and he takes people with him. Yet I was curious. Why, I wondered, was he so affected by someone who was obviously drunk and whose words, if they had relevance to anyone, were aimed directly at himself?

11

Spring has broken like a wave. Fingers of green are seeping out of the grey bark of trees. Yesterday, the air was thick – warm and steamy. Dajti mountain was obscured by a paste of cloud and the air was damp and clammy, soft breath against the skin. The Rruga Sami Frasheri is lined with chestnut trees, which are just beginning to sprout their thick-fingered leaves. This has transformed it into an avenue of sudden beauty, unexpected and ill-prepared for. Its generosity leans on your own heart and you see sunlight in the cracks of the old buildings, you see a tentative history, the embers of something that could be loved. Once upon a time, someone planted these trees, there was pride in the Rruga Sami Frasheri, there was tenderness even.

*

At 8.30 in the morning I'm out on the balcony looking towards the east, up Abdyl Frasheri, where it intersects with the Boulevard. Beyond that it gets misty and the mountains have a pearly, wraith-like distance. There has to be mystery, always, to beckon you on.

Hot on the balcony, but not so hot outside. I go down in the lift, turn right, walk to the corner of the chestnut-lined FEFAD Bank street – Sami Frasheri – right again, along to the bridge. Just on the corner is a memorial stone, set against the wall. It's recent, bedecked with artificial flowers and a photograph. Underneath the name, the dates are written 1979 – 1999. Twenty years old. Mowed down by a car? Shot by the mafia, or just a bystander caught in some crossfire? I can't read what's written on the stone (in Albanian) so I do not know. But there are too many gravestones in the wrong places, in this country – in the streets, by the sides of the roads, in winding, unpopulated areas. Bunches of startling colourful flowers against a backdrop of slate grey or dusty yellow limestone mountains.

*

We drive to Kruje. Cara is a red-haired Australian who runs the Finance Office with professionalism and plenty of humour. I go for a coffee with her, then we stroll round some of the wooden-fronted shops in the cobbled street of the bazaar. In one shop which sells musical instruments there are several mandolins and tambourines. The rings on the sides of the tambourines are made from scrap metal which has been beaten flat. Fragments of letters spell out their origin – *Pepsi, Seven Up, Lipton Ice Tea.*

The last time I went to Kruje there were several KFOR trucks filled with Italian soldiers who were doing some sightseeing up in the Museum. There are not so many people today but the same boy as last time tries to sell me postcards. As we climb the hill to the town we pass a donkey so laden with hay that it is completely covered and only its face is visible in the front.

Just south of Kruje Al spots a rocky cliff set back from the road, about forty-five metres high. We're going abseiling again.

*

Al ties the rope round the tree, clips on the carabiner. The harness is round my waist. He clips me onto the other end of the rope.

Even if you slip now you're safe, he says. You're attached to the rope, you can't fall.

I put on the gloves. My hands are shaking.

You're sure that tree's strong enough? Did you speak to it first? Did you ask it if it was OK to do this?

Of course, says Al. Anything to reassure me.

The rock is sheer down to the bottom, a small level patch where the cars are parked. But on the other side of the road the land plunges down into the valley, so it seems as if you're high above the world.

The rope is looped through the metal descender, then through the carabiner, which is closed and screwed shut. And off I go. One tentative step, then the next. Little rocks are dislodged by the rope and hurtle down. One hits me on the shoulder, surprisingly hard. Cara makes encouraging noises, from the bottom. Dave shouts instructions – let the rope take your weight, lean back – don't bend your legs. Or is he saying bend your legs? I'm not sure. I try to straighten them but then I feel far out in space, suspended in nothing and my knees automatically bend again to bring me closer to the rock. As I move, the rope rubs against the rock. I remember all these films with heroes dangling from cliffs, and close-up shots of the rope which they're attached to, rubbing against a sharp rock and fraying, strand by strand. I put them out of my mind, concentrate on the next step. Little green plants grow from crevices in the rock. I look up. Because of the slight bulge at the top, Al cannot see me or me him. There's just this grey rock and black rope and a tree. I can't see the bottom of the tree where the rope is attached.

I don't look down, except for an occasional glance just beyond my feet to see where I'm going. I looked down once and it was too far, too far still to go. About half way down my arms ached. I imagined I was keeping myself from falling, sliding out of control, by hanging on to the rope with my right hand, pressed behind my back. This was true in a sense but it was also stopping me from moving. When I moved my right hand out and away from my body, while clutching tightly onto the rope with my left one, I moved down a few inches, then put my right hand behind my back again, quickly. My main fear was of the rope slipping through my right hand and me plunging downwards, crashing down and landing on my back. I don't suppose that could have happened. Dave was acting as brake, that would not be possible, but the rational mind was not operating this far above the ground.

About half way down, I stopped. The sky was so blue and the grainy rock-face indented, ridged, changing colour from yellowish-white, like a winter sun, to marbled granite veined with lines of black. The sun was behind me. But I was only aware of tufts of green and grey rock in front of me and the way my hands ached from gripping the rope so tightly. That was the point where fear took hold of me and I froze, unable to move. The realization that only through movement was I going to end this ordeal, forced my hands and feet to move again. I remembered nothing about the second half but when I finally got to the bottom, Dave and Cara cheered and clapped. Dave unclipped the rope from the carabiner round my waist and I took off the harness. I'd done it.

Cara and I sat on the gravelly rocks at the bottom while others – like Al and Dave – ran down the rock-face like goats. Cara is leaving in a few days. She did not choose to, but her contract ends and it was not renewed. Dave's just come back from leave, staying with his wife and daughter, in France. The sun hangs over the valley, like a solitary, fevered jewel.

A couple of children have come over to watch us. Gramoz, our driver, talks to them. Gramoz is a geologist, but he's now studying law and in his third year. There are no jobs for geologists, he explains. A car pulls up on the other side of the road and watches us. Albanians are like that. If they see something going on, they have no hesitation about stopping and watching. The children are particularly open in their curiosity. They can't speak to you, but they stare at you as if you were from some other star-system. They come up close to you.

This happened when we visited Mejda railway station, near Shkodra. There were vendors' stalls on the platform, which looked deserted and abandoned, and there was one old train standing in the station. Its paint was peeling, it was rusty and neglected, but looked as though it might still be able to function. The woman who had the fruit stall was accompanied by two little girls, who crept up to me and followed me into the train, standing beside me on tiptoes to lean out of the train window. The boss took a

photo of the three of us and the smallest girl presented me
with an orange and apple before I left.

Kruje sits on the side of the mountain and the road
twists and winds as it approaches. Pine trees line the road
and gather on top of the granite knolls. The valley hangs
in a pale blue mist.

12

I'm going to have lunch with Steve and Susan. I walk up
Abdyl Frasheri towards the Boulevard, cross over, and
cut through the pedestrian lane that leads to their street.
Their new apartment is one of Tirana's older buildings,
a detached house, divided into two. It has a large garden
with a high wall and a locked metal gate separating it
from the street. They moved to their new apartment after
their holiday in England. Steve said he specifically chose
this house because it was on the ground floor and so it
would be safer in the event of an earthquake.

There is a brief discussion about where to go, but
the final decision is made by Susan who recommends a
restaurant that neither Steve nor I have been to before.
Unfortunately it does not serve pizza and Steve bitches a
bit about this and Susan gets cross.

Well, I didn't know that pizza's not on the menu, you
don't have to get at me, she replies.

That little tiff over, we get down to the juicy gossip.
Steve explains that because this is such a 'hot' place,
intelligence agencies of Western countries are interested
in what goes on.

So – it's logical he says, that in our organisation, there's going to be some people here who are – to put it bluntly – spies.

We enjoy ourselves going through the credentials of the most likely suspects. He tells me a story about someone who was employed here by another NGO. This person, he says, was a bit of a bumbler, he was careless, he knocked things over. He also could not speak a word of any foreign language. But one day he was seen and overheard, speaking to different foreigners – an Iraqi and an Egyptian – and he was conversing in their language. So his cover was blown. His bumbling ways and inability to speak other languages was just a front.

For someone like that, Steve says, they've got to blend in, not look conspicuous, they've got to have a front and his was his awkwardness and his lack of foreign languages, but that was all it was, a front, an act.

*

People talk to me now in the street. Two months ago I felt I had green antennae protruding from my head, the way people stared at me. Now, they think I'm Albanian – or some do anyway. I feel I blend in, at least on the surface, at least visually, I have become part of the patterns of sunlight and shade, covered with a light film of dust. Of course, this visual illusion is dispelled, as soon as I open my mouth and reply in a mixture of Italian and Albanian. But perhaps something more subtle than language has crept into my skin – a tone, a softening or a clarity, a familiarity and sun-warmed affinity with streets, pavements, buildings, shopkeepers and vendors.

Chestnut avenue – Rruga Sami Frasheri – is

turning green as all the trees come into leaf, a glorious transformation, contrasting with the greys and browns of pavements mud and buildings. I'm becoming used to this street, to enjoying the scents of coffee in the morning, and the scents of oil and hot salted cheese and garlic in the evening. In the mornings I turn right when I leave the flat, past the verandah café with its beige awning, past the Irish bar and the *pasticceria* and the woman who almost always sits there – sometimes squatting by the pavement, smoking a thick-boled pipe – wearing block heels and a black coat, her skin brown from exposure to sun and wind and rain.

I go on past little kiosks and litter bins, sometimes burning, at the side of the road. The burning contents are often plastic and rubber refuse which smells acrid, but sometimes it's wood and paper. After passing the rubbish bins I turn right along Rruga Sami Frasheri, avoiding muddy puddles, uncovered manholes, mounds of earth and heaped debris.

13

Cara left today.

The first part of the morning was spent writing a letter for the boss, to the US Embassy. After that I went in the car with the Community Development Officers to the Stefan Centre, where they were being given a day's training. I'd agreed to do a relaxation exercise with them and they seemed to enjoy the guided visualisation. Afterwards, I had an espresso sitting on the terrace of the Stefan Centre, then walked back to the office. As soon as I got there I had to work on the letter I was writing for Al, to try to get a reduction on equipment he was buying in Australia, for his Emergency Preparedness program.

I just managed to finish that in time to jump in the car and go to the airport with Cara. We wove from side to side along the pitted roads avoiding potholes and passing horse-drawn carts. The verges erupted with masses of purple flowers. Dajti mountain wore a jaunty cap of cloud. The few large roadside billboards were faded and peeling.

Outside the airport a few planes gleamed in the sunlight. A crowd was milling around but a policeman stood at the entrance, exercising control by not letting people in until he decided it was permitted. And even when people were allowed in, he checked tickets and turned away those who were not travelling. I got in with Cara because she waved her passport and talked in English and he shrugged his shoulders. I went with her to the baggage check-in then she told me not to wait with her because the plane was bound to be delayed.

Gramoz and I drove back to Tirana in silence.

*

I'm thankful for the sun coming up behind the mountains, slipping behind a long thin barrel of a cloud, and splitting into a curtain of light. And for the trees on Abdyl Frasheri, coming into delicate green leaf.

What is that particular energy that's in the air, that's around, just *there*, yet is absent in Western Europe? It's there in the way people look at you but also in the way they walk, the way they move, aware of everything around them, taking it in, rather than rushing to be somewhere else. At first I felt the way they looked at me was invasive and intrusive and I felt unskinned by it. When I first arrived, walking down any street in Tirana felt like walking into a stranger's living room. People stared at me. I wanted to wander along streets in the way I was used to, looking at what was all around me. But instead of that I found that not only was there very little to feast my eyes on in the Tirana architecture, it seemed as though almost everyone I passed in the streets was looking at *me*. This was not an illusion and not some creeping paranoia. People *were* staring at me. That was what people did, as they walked along the streets. They stared. Not just at me, I soon realised. They just looked. And they talked. When they met people they knew, they stopped where they were on the pavement, greeted each other, started a conversation. It was more like living in a village than a city.

When I walked through the market, eyeing the oranges, bananas, lettuces, tomatoes and the earth-brown olives, the vendors stared at me. At first it seemed hostile. I soon realised that it was not, it was just the way they looked. But it made me feel uncomfortable and awkward. Now, I don't mind it. I wouldn't say I don't notice it but I don't mind it.

A smell of cooking – or wood burning – maybe frying meat, I don't know what it was, but it was definitely Asian – reminded me this is not Asia, not at all. It even gave me a little nostalgia for Asia, the flat bread cooking over palm-leaf and twig fires. So – I might even miss this energy that moves along the narrow pitted streets with you, rubs your shoulder, touches your cheeks, looks into your eyes, as you walk down Rruga Myslym Shyri, with its cafés and restaurants, its *byrek* and *sufflaq* stalls.

14

We were having morning coffee in the café just below the apartment block and Lukas said this was the place where the mafia guys hung out and several people had been killed in the past few months, sitting right here, where we were now.

Lukas works for the BBC and is in Tirana to establish and edit a radio soap, *Rruga me Pisha* – Pine Street. The purpose of this is part entertainment, but also part educational. The idea is that difficult topics such as blood feuds, bribery and human rights issues, could be aired and discussed, in the safe setting of fiction. The soap has become extremely popular, with high listener ratings.

Lukas is fair-haired and blue-eyed with an immensely lively mind, scattering his ideas and perceptions in such a humorous way that we are often doubled up with laughter. On the way to Durres, which is today's destination, Lukas lists the 'possible envisaged scenarios' for Albania. Some of them he forgets and the others I can't hear – I'm sitting in the front, beside Dave, and Lukas is right in the back, beside the rear door. But one of them was that it became the dumping-ground for the whole of Europe – everyone dumped their rubbish here. The last was that it was 'hired' whenever anyone wanted to have a war – you'd book it for your battleground, your war zone. The disadvantage to this of course, was that it would put a lot of soldiers out of work – not to mention the UN and all the NGOs. We'd all be out of a job.

Durres beach turns out to have chalky dusty-looking sand, scattered with litter and the remains of half-demolished concrete bunkers. The beach is also a training ground for children learning to drive, so as well as having to watch where you put your feet to avoid stepping on pungent or decaying garbage, you also have to look around you to avoid the unpredictable swerving of vehicles. The sea is decidedly murky-looking.

On the way back, Dave points to a building at the side of the road.

That used to be a textile factory, he says. It still stands but it doesn't function. The building is made up of rows of crumbling façades with broken windows. There are houses standing beside it, some of them opulent mansions, but all of them are empty and windowless. We pass a group of workers who have put down their tools and are sitting round the bottom of a heap of gravel.

Back in Tirana we gather at Olga's, for a meal.

Tirana nights, sighs Lukas. I see this area as being the fashionable part of town, that's where you guys live. You just walk along the street and meet all these people you know and stop to talk.

In the kitchen Lukas quizzes me about writing – how long does it take you to write a poem? How long do you work on it? Do you think the writing you did when you first arrived in Albania is better than what you'll have written at the end of your stay here? I try to answer his questions. He says he's kept a journal since coming here and finds what he wrote at the beginning, incredibly naïve.

When you first see a policeman accept a bribe, you're astonished and amazed. But once you've been here for a while, then you understand a lot more of the complex situation that goes on around the business of accepting bribes, and why they do it. Partly it's the way it's always been done, partly the low wages that they get, and partly too it's the only way to get known to the people who count, and to have any kinds of prospects of promotion. Not to mention the enemies you could make if you don't do things the way everyone else does. And making enemies here can be very dangerous.

You get used to things, inured to things. Used to the horse-drawn carts, the dirty stray dogs, the litter, the acres of rubble. The bent, collapsed, twisted, half-demolished, rusted kiosks. The immensity of the poverty. The chestnut trees on the Rruga Sami Frasheri have roots – somewhere – beneath the broken and tilted pavement tiles.

*

On Sunday morning, I go with Dave, Susan and Steve to Luna Park which is really part of the large area covered by Tirana Park. Near the entrance there are restaurants, cafés and kiosks, but further away it turns into a wood, with only a couple of paths going through it, leading to the lake.

But today we do not walk far. We choose a table in the bright spring sunlight and order cold drinks. Beyond the tables there's a path surrounded by a few trees overlooking a small cage. I go to have a look and discover there's a monkey inside the cage. I stroke its face through the bars. Its eyes are light brown, with an enormity of sadness in them. Even within the cage it cannot go far, for its leg is attached to a chain.

In the afternoon we go to the gardens of the Rogner Hotel. Florian, the owner of the Irish bar, has arranged it through some connection he has with the management of the Rogner, that we can have the use of the swimming pool. Florian and Lukas actually go into the water. Some of the others – Chris, Steve, Dave and Charlie – are playing tennis. The long leaves of the palm trees flap and crackle in the wind, like distant helicopters. Flip-flip – flip-crackle. The lovely Olga, body perfect in every inch, every muscle, says she's worried she's getting cellulite – does it show? she asks me. She lounges by the poolside in a bikini and I sit beside a palm tree, listening to its stuttering, sibilant talk.

The Road South

Saranda is the jewel of our sea coast.
Naum Prifti

1

Before it became part of the Ottoman Empire, Albania was a Christian country, Catholic in the north and Orthodox in the south, where it borders with Greece. Conversions to Islam took place during the time of Turkish rule, which was established in Albania by the 15th century.

The Ottoman Empire had begun to encroach on Balkan territories during the late 14th century, and there had been raids into parts of Serbia and Albania even before the famous battle of Kosovo Polje in 1389. At this time the Balkan lands were divided into different principalities, often involved in struggles for power with their neighbours. While this lack of cohesion was doubtless a factor in the eventual spread of the Ottoman power, the Turkish threat was certainly recognised and many different Balkan nationalities, which had previously contended for power among themselves, joined forces on the plain of the Blackbirds (Kosovo Polje) to try to defeat the Turkish army. However uncertain the outcome of this battle may have been, it destroyed any semblance of unity among the Balkan armies, and paved the way for the powerful Ottoman forces to spread further into Balkan territories. Serbia, Bosnia, Macedonia, Albania and Greece succumbed and came under the rule of the Sultan, with his seat of government known as The Sublime Porte, from the massive archway leading into his palace and administrative headquarters in Istanbul.

The Balkan peoples never took kindly to Ottoman rule however, and the centuries that followed were peppered with revolts and uprisings against the Turks. These tended to be put down with ferocity. Turkey had some very unpleasant ways of torturing and killing the leaders of rebellions, *'pour encourager les autres'*.

Albania's most famous hero, Scanderbeg (Gjergj Kastriot) led a rebellion against the Turks and held out against them for twenty-five years, an unparalleled achievement in the centuries of Ottoman rule. His clearly charismatic leadership must have been an important factor in this success. Following his death in 1468 however, the rebellion was put down. But Scanderbeg has been immortalised in the Albanian consciousness and his statue is placed in a prominent position in Tirana's main square, which is named after him.

Conversion to Islam took place for different reasons. Albania's feudal society of this time meant that if the leader of a clan decided to convert, all the clan members usually followed suit. Conversion could bring tax benefits (Christians on the whole were not persecuted because of their religion, but they were subjected to extra taxes) and in a rigidly hierarchical society, converts to Islam enjoyed social as well as economic benefits. Another reason for conversion (according to Dora d'Istria's essay – *La*

Nationalité Albanaise) was to do with 'belief following the sword'. In other words, some clan chiefs felt that the god of the Muslim faith must be stronger than the one of the Christian faith, for no god would willingly allow itself to be defeated. Since they clearly wanted to align themselves with the stronger god, they then felt obliged to convert. But a proportion of the Christians had no intention of ever renouncing their faith and were prepared to suffer economic and social deprivation, and sometimes harassment and extreme pressure, rather than convert to the religion of the enemy.

And so, over the centuries, the customs and practices of the Muslim faith took root in a sizeable proportion of the Albanian people. Although it could be said of very few of them that they actually exercised any measure of free choice, but did what they were ordered to do by their leaders or clan chiefs, there is nothing new in religion being adopted at sword point or by necessity. Only kings, clan chiefs and other rulers and leaders seemed to enjoy the freedom of choice of religion and even then, might one day have to put their lives – and those of their followers – on the line and fight with others to defend that choice.

Five centuries later, when the Balkan wars were being fought against the declining Ottoman Empire, 'the sick man of Europe', and Albania became independent, the Muslim religion was very much part of the fabric of their society. After World War II Albania became a communist state, under the leadership of Enver Hoxha. The dictatorship decreed that the country would be an atheist state, with the practice of religion forbidden. Mosques and churches were closed, or used for secular purposes, including in some cases, barns to house sheep or cattle. A huge number of these beautiful and irreplaceable buildings were defaced and even destroyed. To find an old church or mosque in Albania is like stumbling on an unexpected jewel. But now, after the decades of communist rule, there are many ongoing restoration projects, which are slowly piecing together what remains of their rich cultural heritage. Suppression of religion of course does not necessarily destroy it, although the eradication of religious practices can certainly have a strong effect on people's faith and lives. For some, their faith simply went underground, while for others, the purpose of religion disappeared along with the practices.

Juli, a young woman in her twenties, talked to me about growing up in a country which had banned religion.

We do not know the history of religions, she said, we do not know the Bible or the stories from it or the characters. Religion was denigrated when we were in school, it was scorned, and so it never became part of our education.

When I asked her what her parents' thoughts were about religion, she wrinkled her brow.

They did not talk about it she said, because it was too dangerous. People could not even talk to their children about religion, because children might say things inadvertently that could get their parents into trouble. But my grandparents, they were religious, before the communists came to power. They were so unhappy at the ban on religion. When the church they used to worship in was closed, they took the altar from the church, took it somewhere outside the town and they would go there, hold services there, outside. My mother only told me this later, after the communist regime fell. I do remember one time going into my grandfather's room, finding him on his knees, talking. Who was grandfather talking to, I asked my mother. Oh he was just talking to himself she said.

Now of course, I realise he was praying but there was so much that simply was not talked about, when we were young.

Today, according to the statistics, the population of Albania is roughly 70% Muslim and 30% Christian, divided between Catholic and Orthodox.

Many new churches and mosques have been built in the past few years since the communist ban was lifted. With the new freedom to pursue religious beliefs and practices, many older people have returned to their former religion, while many younger ones, with little interest in these systems of belief, would call themselves Christian or Muslim according to what had been traditional in their family, in much the same way that many of us in the West call ourselves Christian, but are not members of a Church. So for many, a religious label is something that is more connected with one's clan or family tradition, rather than with personal beliefs that one has studied, considered and then made a conscious choice to adopt. One is born into a religion it seems, as one is born into a nation. Many Albanians are not fervent believers but have re-adopted the religious label that they inherited from their family.

Nevertheless, there has been something of a religious revival, much of it encouraged and financed by foreign evangelists keen to recruit new adherents. The building of new mosques has been funded by such countries as Turkey and Saudi Arabia while various Christian sects, including Jehovah's Witnesses, Mormons and Baptists, have provided funds for churches and made new recruits, especially among the young, who grew up without any knowledge or understanding of religious beliefs, their place in history, their purposes or practices. For some young people, religion is an exciting discovery and adventure.

My overall impression however, is that particularly among the older generations, Albanians are not rushing to renew religious faiths and practices. For most of these people now it seems, membership of a religion is nominal, rather than arising from profound belief and committed practice.

As freedom to practice religion has been restored, the major Muslim and Christian festivals have been revived and are celebrated by different portions of the population. This year, the Catholic and Orthodox Easter festivals fell on different weekends and we were given a couple of days holiday on the first one, the Catholic one. We intended to make the most of the time off, and planned to explore the south of Albania, which none of us apart from Lukas had visited before.

There were to be two cars going, the second one leaving on Saturday morning. I decided to go with Dave, Lukas and Anna in the first one, which left on Friday afternoon.

The first stop was on the outskirts of the city, to pick up a case of Tirana beer. The second was in Fier, where we met up with some colleagues from the Fier field office. We also bought some food – cheese, ham, olives, cucumber pickles and bread, and made sandwiches to eat on the way.

Our goal for the first night was Dhermis. Lukas had already been there a few weeks ago. He also brought a map with him, and was congratulated on this piece of foresight.

Shortly after leaving Fier, it got dark. After Vlore we climbed up into the mountains, the coast road cutting a thin swathe through towering pines, and winding down again in loops and coils, doubling back on itself like an exploratory snake. We could see nothing beyond the car headlights, just the fringes and outlines of tall trees, the uncertain edges of the road. But as we climbed, the air smelled fresh, it had that mountain scent to it, clarity mixed with the resinous scent of pines, an inebriation you feel sure could bring you swift enlightenment, if you were to spend some time here. However, we had been warned of possible outcomes other than enlightenment, if you spent time on your own in the mountains of Albania after dark, so we did not linger. We got out of the car at the highest point, the Llogara Pass, where the land slopes steeply down to the sea. After that, the road began its circuitous descent.

We heard a soft hooting sound – clear and pure, like a flute played by an adept, and so regular it could have been a decoy, a set trap, a record stuck in a groove to lure us into the woods and to whatever unknown fate might await all travellers irresistibly drawn towards the haunting sound. Lukas told us that this is the sound of the djohn-djohn bird. The story goes that there were once two birds, inseparable as Castor and Pollux, but that something happened to one of them, it disappeared, perhaps to some celestial abode, as in the twin stars, leaving the other calling endlessly, repetitively, for its lost companion.

Dhermis seems deserted when we get there, but we knock on the hotel door and get rooms for the night. We are the only visitors for the tourist season has not begun yet. We leave our bags there and follow Lukas along a dark tree-lined path, a few meters away from the sea. At the end of this path, Lukas knocks on another door. This is the restaurant, he says, where he ate last time he was here. Although it is about ten o'clock in the evening, the restaurant owners show true Albanian hospitality, setting up a table for us outside, with the sea lapping and hissing in a languorous, unhurried way, just below us. We are served a magnificent meal of fish and salad, washed down by Albanian Merlot.

We make our way back to the hotel, along the dark path, accompanied by the sound of breaking waves and the foamy-white gleam of the surf-edge visible in the dimmed light of a half Moon.

2

The main part of the village of Dhermis is near the top of the mountain and a steep winding road runs from there down to the sea. In the morning we drive away from the coastal part of the village and stop about half way up the road. Hidden by trees bushes and undergrowth, there is a tiny old church, an Orthodox cross on its roof, its wooden door latched with a piece of wire. This small church has escaped destruction or defacement. It has suffered from neglect and some of the lovely frescos are half-effaced by damp. But there are signs of human presence and care and an attempt at restoration on the walls.

The coast road from Dhermis to Saranda winds through the mountains. The earth is sienna-coloured, there are terraces of olives, as well as jasmine and lemon trees. Groups of goats appear on the mountainsides, sometimes very close to the road. They have bells round their necks. The sound of these bells is hung on silence like a ripple travelling through the air.

Turning off the road onto a track, we follow it until it vanishes in stones and bushes. A truck is gouging out a path on the slope going down to the sea. Lukas practices his Albanian and talks to one of the men. It turns out that a road is going to be made, leading down to the beach, where a restaurant will be built. The would-be restaurateur, who is currently organising the road building, seems happy and animated. We walk down to this beach and discover an astonishing glade, just behind the short strip of sand.

The grass is so thickly covered with daisies that it looks uniformly white from a few metres away. Terraced layers stir memories of cultivation. The trees and the ruins of buildings feel inhabited by spirits that are at home here, on the earth. The past is so palpable it is almost visible. The feeling is of an old Greek temple, a secluded sanctuary. Behind these gardens is a gorge, sheer red rock going straight up on either side of what was once a river bed. Now it's just a stony trail between the rock walls, flattening and widening as it approaches the sea.

In a short time this glade of secret sanctuary will be desecrated to make room for a restaurant. We get the feeling that we are among the last ever to see this place.

Further down the coast, we visit one of Ali Pasha's palaces, a 19th century building, now abandoned. The path from the road is difficult to make out, as it's thickly overgrown with grass and bushes virtually obliterating it. It's clear that this castle is not a popular tourist resort. Once inside the high stone entrance arch, there are steps leading down into the earth and away from the light; rounding some corners it is pitch black, completely devoid of light. The rooms lead off from one another, in a Turkish-style warren. Faint light filters through from a small hole in the ceiling. In one room the stone wall is pitted with bullet-holes.

Ali Pasha was a native Albanian, nominally an official of the Ottoman Empire, in actuality a despotic ruler of the whole of southern Albania and Epiros, an area that covered what is now southern Albania and northern

Greece, and whose capital was Jannina. Byron had met him and gives a long description of him and his palace in *Childe Harold's Pilgrimage*, saying that Ali

... with a bloody hand
He sways a nation, turbulent and bold.

Byron was keen to meet this legendary ruler, and when he travelled to Greece and Albania in 1809, he went to Jannina for the express purpose of coming face to face with Ali Pasha. Ali was not there, he was currently at war with a neighbouring Pasha and was based at Tepelene, near Gjirokaster, where he had another palace. But news had reached Ali that a young English lord wished to see him and he sent an invitation to Byron to come to Tepelene. So Byron and his companion Hobhouse travelled on horseback across mountainous country – which was also dangerous, because of Ali's ongoing war. Byron describes his first glimpse of the war lord's palace in *Childe Harold*, and it's clear that this mountainous location and its ruler made a huge impression on him. It was after meeting Ali Pasha that Byron was inspired to write his famous poem. So this encounter was crucial, a turning point in Byron's life, for it was the reception of *Childe Harold* by the English public after his return to London, that made Byron utter his historical phrase 'I woke up one morning and found I was famous.'

Lukas meanwhile, regales us with stories of Ali's cruelty – how he would sometimes get rid of his whole harem, and then replace it – not just with women but with children of both sexes as well. Some of his victims were fed to his pet tiger, some were pushed over cliffs into the sea, some were tortured first, many were simply shot.

Whether such stories were true or not, it is known that Ali conducted many savage campaigns, particularly against the mountain Suliotes, who were Christians. These astonishing people, defending every inch of their land, were only finally defeated by trickery. The women and children hurled themselves off the mountainsides rather than be taken captive by Ali and his men. But in 1821 the Greek War of Independence began, and Ali Pasha was playing off allegiances like the independent ruler that he was. This display of power and autonomy became too much for the Ottoman Sultan, and after a long siege and fierce resistance, Ali Pasha's defences were breached and he, now an old man, was put to death in his hideout on the island in the lake of Jannina.

We climb up onto the huge roof, overlooking the sea. A variety of plants and flowers are flourishing all over the cracked and broken roof flagstones. The building is derelict and uncared for. There is much in Albania's history that is abandoned and lost through what seems to be a wilful rejection. Yet so much of their past history feels like an imposition, that the sinking of the past into ruin, its gradual concealment beneath scrub, bush, trees and wild flowers, could seem in some ways, a relief. For who would want to preserve memories of cruelty torture and murder? Then I remember the Greek grove that's about to be ripped up. Mosques and churches that were destroyed and defaced. In the absence of any obvious logic, stories surface, not because they claim dominion, but because they climb into the realm of metaphor and imagination which always commands a grander view than logic. We sit on the roof of Ali Pasha's palace, soaked in sunlight and silence, with just the buzzing of the flies and insects tugging at the edges of imagination, slipping dream focus under our eyelids as we look out at the deep lapis sea, sprinkled with points of light as if fallen from the seed bag of some giant Light Sower, the gods' story teller.

We climb down the steps again into the gloomy warren underneath, before emerging into sunlight and walking back to the road. The dense vegetation on the path springs back after we've passed through, as if determined to erase all signs or tracks of our visit.

At Qiperia, on the way to Saranda, someone flags us down. It turns out that his truck is parked a short way off the road, and at the bottom of an incline. It won't start and his request is that we tow it to the top of the hill, so he can then let it run downhill, and hopefully get it started. Although this is one of the main roads south, like all roads in Albania, it is full of potholes and is crumbling at the edges, which have no barriers to demarcate road from precipitous mountainside. We have been driving for hours but have only met two other vehicles, so it's not exactly the Easter rush from the cities. The person needing a tow could have waited a long time.

We give him a lift to his truck and discover, as is usual in Albania, that this is no solitary enterprise, but seems to have involved not just residents of the cluster of houses, but those from further afield as well. A whole crowd of people are grouped around the truck. There's a lot of talk in Albanian which I don't understand, then someone speaks English. He's an older man, and says he's a doctor. When I say I'm from Scotland, he says that the Scottish and Albanian peoples were one, way back, a long time ago, before the time of Christ, he says. Unfortunately, his English is not good enough to enlarge on this tantalizing snippet of information.

Once the truck has been roped to ours and pulled to the top of the rise, it free-wheels down the other side, coughs, chugs, spits, and then grumbles into life. Lots of cheering and hand-waving accompanies our departure. As we drive along we do not meet any cars, but we do pass the occasional person or group of people, who stare at us. People always stare of course but after a while, Lukas can contain himself no longer.

Look at us! he shouts – feast your eyes on us – four pale-skinned people in a car!

Our next stop is near a small church visible from the road. We get out and walk across the field towards it. But it does not reveal the kind of treasure of the small church near Dhermis. The inside is completely bare and it looks as though it has been used as a barn. On the way back to the car we meet a shepherd, carrying a lamb. Lukas stops and talks to him and he walks back with us to the car. When we get there, we discover that a crowd has gathered. From a landscape that appeared deserted apart from the shepherd, people have suddenly appeared as if they'd been hiding behind rocks, just waiting for our arrival. Within minutes, another car appears, stops, and more people pile out. Lots of hand-shaking goes on. Although we've never met these people before, the feeling is of meeting up with old friends. Lukas is delighted to discover that the shepherd listens to his Albanian radio soap – *Rruga me Pisha*. He rummages in the back of the car for posters he just happens to have brought with him. After extracting ourselves from lots of Albanian bear hugs and kisses, we drive off, leaving the shepherd in the middle of the road, clutching six posters.

We arrive in Saranda in the early evening, find rooms in a hotel and go to eat in a restaurant perched over the sea. We are joined by Arni, who manages the Butrint Heritage Site, and his archaeologist house guests, who are taking part in the ongoing dig and research at Butrint. We also meet Valbona, whose Albanian parents settled in America during the Hoxha dictatorship, after World War II. She was born there but has come back to Albania to live.

Valbona's friend Russell, who is also staying in our hotel, is a large American from Orange County, California. He is the director of the Albanian-American Enterprise Company whose aim is to set up and encourage business.

I'm here to make a praafit – as Dave and Lukas mimic him afterwards. Back at the hotel, we're talking to Russell and Valbona, and drinking some of the crate of beer we picked up before we left.

Do you know what they put in the beer? Russell asks. I shake my head. Formaldehyde, he says. You can feel it at the back of your throat, a hot feeling. He's right, I can. Maybe it's pure suggestion, but feel it I do, and I decline any more of the Tirana beer. Dave and Lukas are less suggestible, question this, laugh, and keep on drinking. Russell smiles too, but has a look on his face that suggests he knows what he's talking about but if these youngsters are not going to listen to him, it's their loss. This country has so many half-digested myths, so many rumours, so much hearsay, and so much conflicting evidence that truth becomes a concept you cannot put a lid on or draw a fence around. People who are good at getting to the bottom of things would probably be able to find truth's secretive lair but mostly, we shrug our shoulders and live in the warm wind of rumour, breathe it in and exhale it as well, trusting in the sunlight and the climate and nature's continued activity to shelter us.

In the morning, I go for a walk through Saranda, looking for a hat. With the advent of hot weather, it's time to find some shady head-wear. I do not find any hats for sale in Saranda, which surprises me, it being by the sea and probably being a holiday resort in the summer.

I can lend you a hat, Valbona says later, when I meet her in a café, near Arni's house. I brought an extra one with me. And she fetches me a red baseball cap.

Later in the morning we go with Valbona and Russell to see the ruins of Butrint, which were only uncovered in the 1930s. Butrint was apparently mentioned in Virgil's *Aeneid* which suggested to the Italian government of the time, the strong possibility of it being an ancient settlement and so, the likelihood of uncovering classical remains. Italy at that time was increasing its influence over Albania, prior to its annexation by Mussolini's government in 1939. The archaeologists began to uncover a host of lost treasures. Their work was interrupted by World War II and though it later resumed it was really only when the Butrint Foundation was established in the 1990s that the site became a protected area and attracted international interest and funding.

The ruins date from different periods. There are solid Illyrian walls from the 4th century BC, the amphitheatre dates from the 3rd century BC, as does a temple of Asklepios. There are ruins of an early Christian baptistry as well as the dramatic, skeletal arches of an early Christian church.

Valbona walks along the path beside the castle walls. The castle is not an old building, not compared to the ancient classical ruins that line Butrint – in rows, in semi-circles, in rectangles. Proud and crumpled ghosts, they evoke wonder, sadness, curiosity and silence. Insects hum and tick, staccato noises and long trails that fade out into a world of dream. I walk a few paces behind Valbona. She walks gracefully, at ease with heat and sunshine and the earth she places her feet on. Russell, walking beside her, has an almost military march in comparison. He is bulky, but not flabby. He treats her with attentive, avuncular care.

Valbona talks gracefully too, she slides her words into the air, she lifts her words to the sun, when she tilts her head and shades her eyes. She does not *waste* words, not ever. She does not scatter them in a torrent, as if they were easily replaceable. She uses them carefully and kindly and they reciprocate.

We walk in silence along the path that leads to the Lion Gate of Butrint. The insects dance and hover and sing in the still air. The Lion Gate is a low doorway, dating from Illyrian times, huge slabs of stonework, as if designed to challenge time itself. We follow the path round to where it skirts the water's edge, then head for the amphitheatre, via rows of arches of an early Christian church, the circular remains of a baptistry and the foundations of Roman baths. Silence hangs as heavy as the creepers and the undergrowth. The curving stone seats of the amphitheatre are waiting, in the sun. I think that one night I would like to sleep on these stone steps and listen to what they heard, all these hundreds of years ago.

The stage is underwater. A large turquoise dragonfly hovers over the surface. Valbona is organising a concert of Albanian flute music to be performed here in the amphitheatre in two weeks time. She wonders if she should provide cushions for people to sit on.

The stone ruins are restful, like an old, old grandfather, whose bones are soaked with memories. These stones have seen and heard and touched so much of life that they have lost that slick human art of judgement. They are much too wise for that. These ruins accept you in the way the stars do. They see you far more clearly than you can imagine. And they wrap their stony arms and their uncoloured light, around you.

Russell thinks the drainage of the stage area will be a problem. He has the air of someone who is used to being listened to and used to being right. Arni has said it will not be a problem. Russell thinks the problem is insuperable and an upper stage will have to be built.

The dragonfly hovers on the water surface. Voices from the stage resonate and sing, caught up in the amphitheatre's arms and raying out into the sky and on to where the light shrinks and darkness swallows sound.

Back in Saranda, in the evening, the air is thick with the scent of jasmine and orange blossom. There's the sound of crickets – the first I've heard this year. The air is damp and warm, sea-damp, wonderful clammy weather. There's a salty smell in the air, the constant sound of the waves, and strings of shivery ropes of green and yellow lights on the water.

Florian, Olga, Jean-Paul and Charlie were supposed to join us on this trip, in a second car. But Dave finds that his mobile isn't working and so we cannot get in touch with them. The further south we go, the less likely I feel it is, that we'll meet up with them.

3

We drive from Saranda to Gjirokaster. The mountains on each side of the road are decorated with seams of angled layers, like rock-cake. The road turns backwards and forwards, sweeping upwards in a succession of hairpin bends, then down again, in a dizzy descent. We stop first near the bottom of a valley. We'd spied a church, half hidden behind trees. We follow a path leading steeply uphill. Trees lean across the trail, which is almost completely covered with undergrowth and bracken. We meet some goats, some black, black and white, some russet. One of them stands on an almost-horizontal tree-trunk, gazing at us as we walk past. From the outside, the little church looks in good condition, its stone walls compact, its orthodox cross intact. But its doors are locked so we cannot see inside.

Our second stop is in a village which is draped in utter silence, like a cloak. All that can be heard is the buzzing of flies. It feels as if everyone has just left. Two large tortoises and a baby one crawl along in the grass beside the stony track to one of the houses. There we come across an inhabitant – an old lady dressed in black, with a white scarf on her head. Her wrinkled face breaks into smiles when Lukas, with his grasp of Albanian, is able to speak to her.

Not far from the village is a steep hill, which the others climb. I go halfway up, then stop. I sit down on the hill-slope, listening to the tinkling of bells – goat bells and cowbells. The heat, the stillness and the sound of bells is mesmerising, both peaceful and profoundly powerful.

When the others come back we head for Gjirokaster. It stands at the head of a plain, between two ridges of mountains. The plain is totally flat, as if it had been scooped out and levelled off. A barge valley. The city of Gjirokaster leans and scrambles up one side of the mountain. The delight of it takes me by surprise. I had not expected this. Old Ottoman buildings fit into the mountainside. They have whitewashed stone and huge wooden beams that lean out from the walls and support the stone-tiled roofs that overhang parts of the buildings, providing shelter and protection from all elements. Their weighty yet elegant structures give a deep sense of durability and time.

Like outcrops of the mountain itself, you feel they are its agents, its accomplices, and their destinies are linked with the rocky land that they have grown out of. Something of dependability and authority in them. Something that has weathered changes we could hardly imagine and that has roots in a perception that is not our own. It started a hunger in me to know it better. To know its layers of history, through direct contact with its stone. To feel its stone beneath my feet and pressed against my palms.

One of the main characters in Ismail Kadare's *Chronicle in Stone* is the city of Gjirokaster itself. He describes it as being *like some prehistoric creature that was now clawing its way up the mountainside.*

His images of wartime and winter are grey and grainy, like old photographs. Kadare is a master of monochrome and this superb and captivating story shimmers like reflections seen in water, constantly breaking up and reassembling. Gjirokaster is bombed first by the allies, (as it is occupied by the Italians,) then by the Italians when it was taken by the Greeks. Flags flying from the city constantly change, as do the nationalities of the bombers.

I am seeing it in spring, when there is no wind, only sunlight pouring down on it, tumbling down the layers of steep stone buildings, edged and cuffed with green lace of bushes, trees and plants.

We stay at Haxhi Kotoni's house, an old Ottoman building, high up on a terraced slope. From the balcony outside our rooms, where I am sitting drinking Turkish coffee – thick, gritty and sweet – I have a clear view of the house opposite. Its framed windows are divided into eight. The slate roofs are connected to the house by slanting wooden supports. The middle part of the house is set back, with a large balcony in the front. This balcony is host to stone or earthenware pots which have green plants growing out of them.

A few meters away from the narrow road that clutches the side of the steep slope where the house is built, the land plunges into a miniature gorge, fringed with treetops. On the other side of the gorge is an old mosque. We visit the oldest Ottoman house, which is now a museum. Taulent, the young son of Haxhi and Rosa, tells us that a film, *Sako's Wedding,* was recently made here.

The house is opened up for us to view. It is almost empty. Its huge ceilings, massive wooden beams and wooden stairways to the upper levels, feel soaked through with time. Its history is tangible, like something you could pull out of the air and take away with you. The wood of the divans and chests is so dark it's almost black. There is dark red fabric on some of the divans and upstairs, there's a fireplace so massive you can walk into it. A huge worn carpet covers the floor, its patterns so dark you can barely make them out, but the intricacy of its designs is still arresting. The balcony gives a panoramic view out over the city. Like many old buildings in Albania, it is due for restoration but when this would begin and how long this process would take nobody could say.

There is something oppressive in this old house, as if the air had grown thick with time. It feels as if movement itself is impeded, inducing torpor and lethargy. You could easily imagine people sitting around the fireplace cross-legged on cushions on the floor, over-arched by the enormous ceiling. But I could not imagine fluidity or movement, laughter or embraces. The house seemed to growl quietly, warning us we had no right to be here, moving around it so freely. But even our movements are slow, we tread softly on the ancient wooden floorboards and speak in hushed voices, as if we have entered someone else's dream.

Taulent is our guide, as we walk down the curving sloped streets, laid with slender polished cobblestones and lit with delicate pale yellow street lights. It is entrancing, this light, shining off the narrow cobbles. It reminds me of Italy's Umbrian towns, with medieval buildings and curling streets, but it is not the same, it holds another quality that I have not come across before. Its restfulness is also an alertness and a vividness, with an undertone of sharpness, that catches at your breath like a sliver of frost tucked inside the softness of the spring night.

Kadare says in *Chronicle in Stone* that anyone seeing Gjirokaster for the first time found that *the city rejected all comparisons*.

And I felt that, walking in its evening streets. Not just its physical appearance but its very breath, its rumour, was something I could find no comparison for. Its emotional map as well as geographical, had a quality all of its own. It twisted your heart as well as allowing you to lean towards it like a song. It stirred discomfiture as well as admiration. I felt immediately that it was a place I wanted to come back to, for it left a hook in me, that stirs sometimes, awakens restlessness, a memory of something missing.

The plain below the city is so flat it reminds me of a chessboard, only thinly populated with pieces as if the players have abandoned it. While the city has an agile energy, the plain looks as if it has been left in some displaced enchantment that it hasn't woken from. It is too flat, too deserted, while the mountainside, heaped with buildings, gives you a ledge and a breathing space and something you can lean against, with gratitude.

Taulent is our guide too, when we go to the citadel, now a museum, on the top of a hill, looking down on the city. It was once a fortress, part of it a prison. We enter from the cavernous and pitch black underground passages. There are old cannons and a tank near the entrance, like guardians, and further on, the darkness is so intense you just see the dim shapes and memories of light that dance against your eyelids when you close your eyes. We take a path that climbs upwards and back to daylight, clamber up steps and over rusting barbed wire that lines the flat roof, and peer through narrow openings down into the cells below. Abandoned cells now, but it was the old prison. Long ago disused, still, we were not supposed to be up there on the roof and the two museum wardens shouted to us angrily. We came down, paid our entrance fee to the museum and walked through the permitted area.

There's very little to see. A few Socialist Realist paintings, and rifles in cases (some cases are empty, where the guns have been stolen). A few traditional clothes – a black sheepskin, wrap-around poncho, embroidered shirts. Racks of paintings from the communist era are stacked behind a screen.

Can we see them? Lukas asks.

No, they're not on view to the public.

But why not? A shrug. There's no space.

They were in the art gallery, but that's closed now. So they lie here, until someone decides what to do with them.

The prison was used in the pre-communist era in the time of King Zog. In one corridor, lino cuts are displayed on the walls. Some of them depict prisoners escaping. There are no signs in the museum, of the communist era.

It might never have existed. Outside on the grass, shining in the spring sunlight, there is a small plane, a MIG, reputedly shot down in the war or shortly afterwards, British or American. The guide doesn't seem to know who the pilot was or what their mission was, or their fate. In the lack of any real knowledge of history, the mountains create their own myths.

We leave the following morning to begin the long drive back to Tirana.

<h1 style="text-align:center">4</h1>

A few days later I was looking in the English language *Albanian Daily News* and noticed that the film *Sako's Wedding* was showing at the Millennium Kinema that evening, for one night only. This was the film Taulent mentioned was shot at the old Ottoman house in Gjirokaster. It was being shown as part of an award-giving ceremony for Balkan film-makers and attendance seemed to be by invitation only, like a private view of an exhibition. However, I persuaded Ylli, one of my Albanian colleagues, to come with me and Dave and Lukas joined us, convinced by my reasoning that if we looked as if we had every right to be there, we would have no problem getting in, which turned out to be the case.

First of all, there were speeches and various people came onto the stage to receive their awards. Despite the speeches which were no doubt fulsome in their praise (though incomprehensible to me) and the applause, the awardees looked neither delighted nor affable, but rather, constrained and suspicious. I wondered if this was because Albanians felt that any public appearance or singling out, even for accolades, brought something dangerous with it as well, waking up from its slumber some dark spirit that did not want to be disturbed. Some chthonic deity that was the underside of this light-filled country, some shadow glued to the light, as securely as the valleys attached themselves to the high mountain ridges.

Whatever the reason, the gainers of awards looked uneasy, as if they had deliberately touched some darkness or some god, whose reactions were unknowable. The mood of gloom was palpable, in the film itself. There, the danger inherent in breaking taboos, was followed by seeming inevitable treachery and revenge.

The dialogue was of course in Albanian, and I was resigned to not being able to understand anything more than how are you, thank you, goodbye etc. But to my delight, there were French subtitles. The backdrop was the majestic scenery of the mountainous region of the south. Most of the action, apart from the very last scene, took place in some unidentifiable time in the past. Colours were sombre – browns, greys and dark greens, matching the mood, which was heavy as a goatskin weighted with wine. Much was made of silences, charged with sensuality and unspoken jealousy. There was no real emotional catharsis, and the sexual consummation of the lovers was implied by the wife's absence rather than any overt sex scene. But even this did not seem to lift any of the weight from a pervasive longing that soaked through the whole fabric of the film. The real consummation was a trick played on the eponymous Sako, peeled back like a partly-exposed knife, heavy with potential violence, an unstated threat which seeped and spread like a stain into all areas of his life.

The old Ottoman house in Gjirokaster was not just the backdrop, but a character, a mood. I recognised its mood from our visit there – sombre and stifling, pressing its own will on the hapless characters, who sat around, almost immobile, weighed down by the thick past that the house emanated like a stupefying drug.

The last part took place in the present time, showing an affluent confident family with charming well-groomed children dressed in colourful modern clothes. Presumably Albanian Americans returning to their home country, they were standing at the balcony of the old house in Gjirokaster, where the action had taken place in the past – the same balcony we had stood on. But the house worked on them like opium as well, turning their present into an evocation of the past, so that it ended in an enigmatic melancholy, full of the longing that still pervades this country and many of the people, as if the past has a weight to it that has settled into the mountains and is never far below the surface.

I felt that the film had told me a lot about the Albanian psyche, with its roots as long and deep and entrenched as the mountain gullies. I liked the way it was underplayed, but it had a lingering feeling of prologue, as if what it really wanted to say was never quite revealed. The future curled back into the past, layered with secrets. It was a little like an unresolved dream, with the present waking life taking place off-stage, in America, where Sako emigrated to. Yet his descendant, returning to Albania, had inherited some kind of racial memory, as well as the national nostalgia which rears like a blister on the psyche when it returns to its place of origin. I wondered about the curious sense of recognition, some unique quality of energy that emanates from the land, which our bodies, created out of the same magnetism and minerals and light, cannot help but respond to, recognising it as part of themselves.

I was delighted with the insights the film presented but Lukas erupted into lyrical condemnation as soon as we were outside.

God it was awful, he said, turgid, slow, nonsensical anathema.

Yet he looked pleased too, as if some suspicion he had harboured for a long time, had been vindicated.

Tirana Nights and the
Ethem Bey Mosque

*A clear night has fallen with its soft, supple body
Upon the great city.*
Natasha Lako

1

The sun comes up over Dajti mountain at 6.15 approximately. I know because it jumps across the rooftops of Tirana, curves round the edge of the balcony, comes through my window and lands on my face.

My three month contract is almost over but I do not want to leave, not now, when spring is opening up the country and its warmth and blossoming is melting something in me too. So I speak to the Country Director and tell him I would like to stay on. To my amazement and delight, he offers me a further four month contract. I leave his office walking on air, feeling quite dizzy with joy to know I would be spending another four months in this country. Ylli and I go for a drink after work to celebrate.

Just after I get home there's a knock on the door and Florian, who lives on the floor above, asks me if I'd like to go for a drink to the Irish bar downstairs. I am bubbling over with my good news. He is pleased for me and the wine and the music all combine to produce a euphoria that follows me out of the bar and into the street and winds itself around me like a creeper as we turn the corner, walking in the soft warmth of the spring night, our footsteps crunching on the dust and gravel leading to the apartment block door.

Once inside, I go onto the balcony and look down onto the pale lights, the winking red and green ones and the soft and wrinkled shadows of trees on the Rruga Abdyl Frasheri. The evening air is soft against my skin and I can hear the faint sounds of frogs.

A police car crawls down the Boulevard, blue lights winking. What am I to do with all this soft and creamy magic, this match-flame of memory, so precarious, so much – nothing at all of any consequence, and still – so much. Faint scents of orange blossom, lights on Dajti mountain, and the flute call of the djohn-djohn bird.

The music is still in my bloodstream along with a sense of something so intimate and pervasive, that I feel I have lost all covering and weight and have turned into night sounds and scents, just music and the shimmering night and nothing more than this.

2

Dajti is shrouded with banks of cloud obscuring any view of the mountain. But here above the streets the sunshine falls like slow points of light. The chestnut blossom on the trees is already beginning to fade a little. Rruga Sami Frasheri has a huge canopy of leaves that spreads out protectively – it is completely transformed. Last night, the woman who sleeps out near the Irish bar lit a small fire of cardboard boxes. A black dog was lying beside her coat.

Early this morning someone was scooping up trash and putting it into the big metal bins. Something acrid is being burned just now, the smell drifting through the open window. I'll soon be flying from Rinas airport, for a week's leave. I feel so thankful I'll be coming back again. To these dusty streets, smoking trash, loud cars and barking dogs. Yet I love it, at least, I do right now.

*

Adem drives me to Rinas airport.

You – come back? he asks, gesticulating with his arm to demonstrate his meaning.

Yes.

Good, he says. He has stuck his cigarette up one nostril, to my surprise. A variant, I suppose, on putting it behind your ear.

At the airport the plane is two hours late in taking off. I have no idea why there is such a delay. We fly over rows and rows of mountains. A few still have streaks of snow on them, like a crust of salt, or dried tears.

And I think – Albania, this young democracy, is like an abused child. It's looking out for its own survival, it can be devious and untrustworthy, because it grew up with communism, not love. Some of the foreigners laugh at it, make jokes about it, are rude and arrogant. Just this morning, driving to work, George was making his usual caustic, arrogant remarks –

So much is *stupid,* he said – then added – but I must admit I'm driving the wrong way down a one-way street.

And so I had to forgive him for his comments. But they still rankled. Yesterday we had a real argument. The boss, for reasons best known to himself, had asked George to work with me, updating the orienteering manual given to all new staff. In the description given of the immigration process at Rinas airport, George wanted to include the word 'inefficient'. I said that was a value judgement and could be considered offensive. He said it was our job in the report, to make value judgements. I said no, it was to report facts and be diplomatic. I called him a cultural chauvinist. I've never been called that before; an arrogant bastard yes, he said. When I explained that it meant roughly the same thing, he liked that, took it as a compliment and laughed, which eased the tension and allowed him to back down without losing face. The interesting thing about George is that, no matter how cutting critical or condemning he may be about Albania or Albanians, he does not appear to take personally any criticisms handed out to him. It just does not reach the part of him that could be hurt – assuming he has such a part. He just grins as if the tight, puckered, drawstring bag of his face, has been suddenly released.

3

Cara lives in Brixton now. On a row of these wonderful London Victorian houses with their bay windows leaning out like a declaration, a tentative gesture towards the street, a mixture of solidarity and shyness, a hand held out to street, a refusal to be kept within the bounds of buildings. Bulgy houses, slightly pregnant.

Her street gives onto a leaf-dappled one, and at the end of that you come out onto a busy London road, full of buses and traffic and people walking purposefully along pavements, striding with intent – black-skinned and brown-skinned and fair-skinned people.

I arrived in Brixton the night before my return flight to Tirana. There were people lying on the pavements, people selling the Big Issue, people shouting that there are tickets for sale for the Paul Weller concert, people watching you, people standing and waiting by the underground, people who ask you for money, people who ask you for cigarettes, people talking on cell phones.

Fuck off you little creep, says a beautiful black girl in a tight short skirt. She says it into her mobile phone. She replaces it in her bag. It rings again. She puts it back to her ear.

Why should I pay for you? You should be paying for me, she says.

I stay the night at Cara's house and leave at five in the morning. The streets are quiet and whispery, the trees still drenched with night, night slipping off their leaves and bunching round their roots, night hunched and hesitant and lying on the pavement cracks like water. Night's geometry of memory, its grid-work of desire, intent, and its sweet hegemony. Night's Cyrillic alphabet, its creamy tiny roots like down on someone's arm.

I take the underground from Brixton to Heathrow. There are no queues at the Malev airline check-in desk. It is raining when we arrive in Budapest, a thin grey drizzle. When we land at Rinas airport the sky is overcast, but there is no rain.

It feels so good to be back home again, sitting on the

balcony, mesmerised by the traffic winding its way up Abdyl Frasheri. The evening light. The deep green of the leaves.

*

I wake to the rain beating madly on corrugated tin. There's a background beating and dripping and a closer drip, drip, sound from the edge of the building. The mad, wild chorus of birds brings memories of a blackbird's song, its intricate melody every morning and evening.

The sound of fierce rain and the feeling of cool air drifting like slow breath, through the open window. The sound of the rain reminds me of a morning in Paris, several years ago. I was leaving that morning, and I woke up to the sound of rain. Sounds and voices carry, in damp air. I heard the usual sounds there – the garbage trucks collecting the bins of refuse from cafés and restaurants. Cafés just opening, steel shutters rattling, wooden ones creaking on their metal hinges, thudding against walls, people calling to one another. A few traffic sounds, one or two motorised scooters. An enormous energy, a huge sense of wonder, a reconnection with that larger life.

Here, the dogs bark, one or two roosters crow and the car tyres hiss on the wet roads. It has stopped raining. It's six o'clock now and the traffic is increasing. Two street sweepers with long brooms are sweeping debris into the sides of the road and along the gutters towards the big metal garbage bins. A scraping sound of someone shovelling debris from the pavement.

Earlier this morning, the frogs were making their light sounds, almost like ducks quacking, but they are silent now.

Night frogs.

What makes a place slip into that larger life, that sense of Presence? I do not know. But it seems to lie in the lowered defences that come about through movement and change of environment – and something to do with the place itself, its *genius loci*, slouching in the wings, waiting to grab your soul and become one with it. Places can be lonely too. Places too, can long for intimacy.

4

I watch the rubbish collectors pull the garbage bins from the pavement. When they open the back of the *saubermacher* truck, a pile of unsifted rubbish falls down onto the street. I couldn't help laughing and neither could they. They took their shovels and just shovelled it up again into the back of the *saubermacher*. The morning streets looked clean and empty, litter free, in the leafy, shaded Rruga Abdyl Frasheri.

There is new paving in the office yard when I get back. The building between Rruga Mujo Ulqinaku and the hole in the wall is progressing by leaps and bounds. Wooden scaffolding has been erected and a bright purple teddy bear is tied to the top of one of the wooden posts to ward off 'The Eye'. There's a wooden fence now on the edge of the muddy lane though there's still a gap at the side, big enough for people to pass through.

I walk home from work along the street with the shop that sells Italian ice-cream, the Rruga Bajram Curri. Through an archway that's half-blocked with overflowing bins and garbage piled beside them, you can see the crumbling reddish, yellowish plaster of older buildings, given a kind of grandeur from their cracked and moulted, peeling outer skin.

Olga and I go to Ravena's café, drink chilled beer. As soon as you touch the glass condensation runs down the side.

I do not know if I want to spend the rest of my life with Jean-Paul, says Olga. He is a good man but there are many things, difficult things – I would like someone – someone who is sensitive, who can listen, not someone who always has to argue and confront you and say the opposite of what you feel. Have you ever felt that there has always been something you wanted in your life, that you have never had? I feel that there has always been someone I've been looking for but I have never found.

Everyone around us is laughing, drinking, enjoying the evening light slowing, dimming, like a long-awaited curtain drawing back, for some stage-set. It occurs to me it's always the anticipation that I feel most, the subtle rising of temperature or rising intent, the erotic play of dark and light.

Back home, out on the balcony, the frog chorus rises and stutters and falls. Perhaps it's the different kind of light, that stimulates different parts of the brain. As well as the land of course, the terrain, the way it cuts into your heart and leaves gaps and edges and scars. There have been sounds tonight like gunfire. Maybe it's just fireworks. Simon says there's been daylight shootings recently in Shkodra. Someone even threw a hand grenade, which fortunately didn't go off.

The sun hovers and drifts, sails and hesitates and plunges down behind the Tirana tower blocks and the wake of all that's left behind stains the sky with elderberry juice, dark plum, burnt cherry.

Now that summer is here, the vines that are woven into trellises form patchwork green coverings over gardens. I caught a whiff of orange blossom in the Rruga Mujo Ulqinaku and Epiros placed its hand over my eyes and the dusty, pitted little track shimmered into groves of orange and jasmine blossom, with the honey-stutters of frogs and the soft winking gleams of lightning bugs.

5

It took me five years Engjellushe Bejtja said, to convince the authorities that it would be far better to give our school an individual name, and a positive one. Schools like ours used to be called simply Handicapped Schools. And many still are. But that name was such a burden. So much has to do with our perception, don't you think? It's taking a long time for perceptions to change in this country. Our biggest hurdle, apart from the lack of funding, is to overcome this way of seeing and of being seen as well.

Engjellushe is a soft-voiced slender woman who radiates an energy of vitality that is both determined and gentle. She is the head teacher of a school in Elbasan for children with learning disabilities. These schools are referred to as Handicapped Schools and this name as Engjellushe points out is part of her struggle to get people to be accepting and understanding of people with such disabilities.

Gramoz, Rudina and I had travelled to Elbasan from Tirana that morning, driving along the road that winds high up into the mountains so that you get an eagle's eye view of mountain peaks, layer after layer shimmering into distance, breathtakingly beautiful in this cloudless morning in early summer. Despite being so high up, the air was still and there was not a breath of wind. In winter, these mountains are coloured every variety of brown, with snow-tipped peaks. But in summer they are covered with green vegetation. As we approached Elbasan, there was a profusion of star-like yellow flowers, waving in the slightest breeze on their long stems. There were herds of goats and a few sheep and cows strolling across the road. Vendors at the roadside sold cherries, plums, orchids, olive oil, from stalls with woven leafy coverings.

The school is in a quiet shady suburb of Elbasan. The gates to the school are of delicate metalwork, the mixture of security, grandeur and beauty that Albania is so good at. Such gates are not the offensive growling barricades that we are used to, their very stance and stature shouting keep out, even if there is no such sign attached to them. On the contrary, their wrought metalwork is alluring and welcoming. The school is located in a large high-ceilinged old building that was donated to them by the Church. There is a yard in the front and a small garden at the back. On the other side of the yard is a small stone church.

The building was lucky to have survived the ravages of the communist hunger for destruction and desecration in the early seventies. Every time you come across an old building in Albania the effect of its beauty is inevitably tinged with poignancy for all the other buildings that have been lost.

Two flights of stone steps zigzag up the outside. Inside, footsteps echo slightly on the flagstones, polished with use, and the building is refreshingly cool, contrasting with the heat outside. The rooms on the ground floor are spacious and high-ceilinged and echo with the buzz of voices and laughter. This is one of the things you come to expect in Albania. This is an occasion of some formality. The greenhouse, funded by the aid organization I work for, is to be officially opened today. As well as the teachers, the priest is in attendance to give the project his blessing and outside in the walled garden, media people and TV cameras jostled for positions.

Engjellushe insisted that I cut the red ribbon, and after the speeches were made and the photographs taken we went back inside and I talked to her in her office upstairs.

But when I speak to Engjellushe on her own, and ask her about the school and her work here, she becomes animated and it is clear that this is much more than just a job to her – she takes a very personal interest in the school's welfare.

Handicapped people were traditionally kept inside, she says, shut away from others and from public life. There was a climate of denial and unspoken social pressure to hide them away as if they were something to be ashamed of.

I have a child with learning disabilities myself, she says, so I know exactly what they suffer and what difficulties are also faced by their families. Her daughter, she tells me, used to attend this school and although she is now too old for school she still comes sometimes, because she enjoys being here. One child, when he first came, he could not walk at all but now he can go about twenty metres on his own. This helps the parents too, she says, his father said that the first day his child was at school, his arm felt strangely light, because he had been so used to supporting him as he walked.

Attitudes towards the disabled are changing, she says,

but they still have a long way to go. My own attitude has changed as well. I used to be almost afraid to go out and my daughter did not like it either, she was aware of people staring at her. But now, I can walk freely with my daughter in the streets, we can go to cafés and drink a coca-cola together and she is happy to go out with me.

And finally, she says, schools can now choose their own names. It took me five years to convince the authorities that 'Handicapped Schools', was a humiliating name. They just didn't understand the importance of the name, how it can change people's perceptions – not just of the children who attend this school and their families, but those of the larger public, who are beginning to see the school and the children in a positive light. But the authorities support me now. So our school's new name is *Zera Jete* which means *Voices Full of Life*.

She also has long-term hopes and plans for the school and the children attending it. With the equipment provided – shovels, trowels and spades – the digging and preparation of the earth around the greenhouse has already begun. Flowers and vegetables will be planted, both within the greenhouse and outside it. She would also like to dry flowers in the greenhouse. If the Education Department agrees, she says they could create a small business from their produce and dried flowers. The money made from this could be used to buy essential items, such as teaching aids and a tape recorder. This could even provide employment for the children once they had finished school. And it would let other people see that these children too, can be useful.

We go downstairs to join the other teachers and guests in the refectory. The tables are groaning with food and there is much animated talk and laughter. Engjellushe and the priest give speeches and toasts are drunk. There is applause, followed by more conversation. Albanians are such lively, vivacious and interested people, so open in their curiosity and enthusiasm that you cannot fail to find their energy both captivating and contagious.

Across the yard from the school the old Orthodox Church with its grey stonework and shady arches casts an atmosphere of serenity. The slender metalwork of the gates is twisted into patterns that throw threads of shade on the dusty ground. Engjellushe and I embrace, before I climb back into the car with Gramoz and Rudina.

6

The lease on the apartment in Abdyl Frasheri has run out and so I'm looking for somewhere else to live. Florian says there's an empty apartment on the floor above and he knows the landlord – would I like to meet up to see it? I say I would. We arrange to meet the next day, at lunch time. Gramoz drives me to Abdyl Frasheri and drops me off opposite the Fitness Centre, where I meet up with Florian.

We go into the apartment block, take the lift up to the top floor, ring the bell and the landlord lets us in. He is a tall man, well-built, possibly in his fifties. A delighted energy spills from him. He laughs when he takes my hand and gestures around the apartment.

I cross the large living room and go out onto the balcony, while he talks to Florian. The view of Abdyl Frasheri is the same. I think of Steve and Susan, now back in Australia. Steve, with his fear of earthquakes, would have been horrified to live so high up. When I go back through, I attempt to converse with the landlord in German, as he claims to speak that *ein bisschen*. He roars with delight at everything I say, but replies in such heavily accented phrases that I find it difficult to understand. I catch *schlafen*, with a questioning tone, as he places his hand on my arm, and I'm not sure if he's talking about the apartment or propositioning me. His energy is infectious but I smile and shake my head, leaving him to interpret that in whatever way he wants. Completely undeterred by this, he laughs again, and hugs me.

What do you think? Florian asks as we take the lift back down.

It's lovely, but the price he's asking is too high. But maybe I'll tell George and Anna – it might suit two people.

＊

Gazim met me outside the Fitness Centre. He grabbed my hand and shook it vigorously. Gazim was going to help me find a new apartment. He gestured towards his car, an embrace of a gesture, taking in as much of his offer or his country, as I could absorb. No limit to what he was prepared to do. He finished every sentence or phrase, with laughter. And he talked a lot. Words bubbled up from him, fed by some underground spring of vitality and delight. His joy was utterly infectious. Nothing brooding, sinister or unknown here. He was the sun's emissary, at home equally in distance or proximity. All the sky was his. He had the knack of light, he was a lodger in the house of Sol and it carried him through all varieties of darkness whether night or mist or rain-bellied cloud. The confidence of light carried him through all of these.

The light was fierce, the sun like a hunter, leaping on your skin as soon as you stepped out of shade. It pounced on you, unleashed from shade of awning or chestnut tree, slapping your skin with shock. Gazim flung his arms wide and I stepped into his dusty Mercedes, with the driver's door half hanging off, the window that refused to wind up and the suspension so shot that it almost scraped the ground and every bump and pothole it went over registered its jarring notes through your whole body. We bumped and rattled our way down Abdyl Frasheri, along Deshmorit and turned down Pjeter Bogdani. He assured me I would like this apartment and I did. The living area was enormous, with lots of light. But the balcony looked out onto an apartment block in the process of construction and so close you could almost reach out and touch it with your hand.

The second one we looked at was between Deshmorit and Vaso Pasha, inside the courtyard of older buildings. It rose up from the middle, like a totem pole. The whole courtyard was a building site, strewn with rubble, broken glass, twisted metal, slats and boards of broken wood. The apartment was on the eighth floor. The living room was not so spacious, but the bedrooms each had their own balcony, with a wonderful view out over the city's rooftops. A sliding glass door out onto the balcony, and a little table to work at.

Gazim pressed my hand and laughed with delight, slapping the steering wheel, when I said I preferred the second one. I could pick up the keys and move in at the end of the week, he said. We slid, ground and jostled our way back to Abdyl Frasheri.

7

The storm comes out of nowhere. The blue sky darkens suddenly like a rising flush of fever. The wind rolls down Dajti mountain with its cloak streaming out behind. It smashes into the high-rise buildings and currents of lights spark in the sky. There's a sound of breaking glass. The sky shouts and growls and the rain rushes in the open window of my new apartment. A magpie hops across a flat roof below me. Some of the older buildings surrounding my new apartment block have flaked plaster, peeled away to reveal the bricks. A yellow light has staged itself behind the hills which drape the horizon, a moist curtain, waiting to be lifted.

The sky shouts again and the light behind the hills illuminates a fairy-world we cannot see. A tiny grey speck in the sky slides through the yellow light – pauses – then turns around, sloping down, falling through the yellow light, metal wings spread, disappears between the tower-blocks and the little, dimpled, cake-icing hills.

*

I ask Bardyl if he knows of Robert Carver's book of his travels in Albania in 1996, *The Accursed Mountains*.

Robert Carver, he says, yes, I met him.

You met him?

Just once. I did some translating for him. When he was in Shkodra, he talked to the president of the society that helps people who were victims of torture in the communist regime. A friend of mine was translating for him. One day my friend was ill, and he asked me if I could do it. So I did, of course. Then I heard that Robert Carver had left. But I've not had any more contact with him.

We are sitting in the booth of a café at the intersection of the Bulevardi Zhane d'Arc and the Rruga Deshmorit – on the other side of the Boulevard is the pedestrian bridge that crosses over to Bajram Curri. We had met at the corner and stood talking. He suggested having a coffee. He tells me he studied fine art at University.

And do you still paint?

He does. He has sold some paintings, he has exhibited in Tirana and Yokohama, Japan. He has been to England – he spent two months in Winchester as the guest of a professor of religion at the university there. This professor is now ninety two years old.

What kind of painting do you do?

Primitive. Painting – you know – is a way of expressing – he lifts his hand briefly to his heart – the spiritual, the emotions.

He looks around him.

Everyone has these feelings, but not everyone has a way of expressing them. Painting – or writing – that is a gift – so it should be used.

Then he says, do you like it in Albania?

I tell him I found it strange at first, but now, it feels like home. We drink espressos and *uje megaz*. We are sitting in the shade. I brush insects off my legs. I cross them, then uncross them. I can feel the insects biting me. I'm wearing shorts. Bardyl is wearing black trousers. He does not shift around. Perhaps the flies don't bite him. He does not twitch or fiddle, the way I do. He sits very still. He has come down from Shkodra, just for the day, to see his aunt. He's travelling back again later today.

He tells me how much things have changed in Albania

in the past decade, but that democracy will take time, it cannot just change overnight.

What's most important to change, is people's mentality.

Education I say, pouring some more *uje* into the glass.

Exactly. That's the only way to change the way people think.

I watch him talking, sometimes searching for the right words.

Do you speak any other languages?

I began learning German but my tutor went away and I stopped. But I would like to take it up again.

Will you be coming up to Shkodra soon? he asks.

Perhaps this week, maybe next. I'll need to speak to Al and see what his plans are and when he's next teaching the Emergency Preparedness class. How is that going?

Very well. Everybody is enjoying it. I do the translating. When you come, will you stay for a few days?

I say I'd like to. I say I'd like to see Shkodra Lake. As well as his paintings. I fiddle with the empty bottle of water.

Would you like another drink?

I say no.

The table is wooden and wobbly. I shift around, flick the flies off my legs. Bardyl sits very still.

I'm not keeping you back?

No, he says. I told my aunt I'd be away for an hour or so. I have to go back to Shkodra tonight because we have a busy day tomorrow.

*

The night lights shiver in the distance. Faint sounds of jazz come from the Berliner restaurant. The night is warm and sticky. From the balcony, the moon is behind wings of cloud, bunched and furred like owl feathers. The sun kisses this land, over and over. I can't sleep. It's hotter than last night. I get up and stand under the shower, with the tap turned to cold. For a few minutes afterwards I feel cool. The clock that Alma, the landlady, bought me, ticks faintly. The lamp she bought me, for reading at night or working at the desk, has a dimmer switch. I throw off the thin sheet. The almond shaped moon has slipped down the sky. There's a few faint stars.

While I'm talking with Bardyl, a ragged child comes over, begging. Bardyl says something quietly to him, but he does not go, he persists. He comes closer to me, touches me lightly on the arm. Bardyl says something else. But he's not giving up. I try to ignore him. Bardyl does too, but he's finding it difficult. In the end, he gives the boy ten lek and he leaves. I'm sorry, says Bardyl. He's embarrassed.

The waitress comes to ask for the money for the coffees. I try to pay but Bardyl is quicker than me and will not let me give him money. Well, next time, I say.

I go through to the kitchen, get some water out of the fridge. Music is still coming from the Berliner. A clarinet plays a funky melody. Some dogs bark.

Bardyl and I shake hands when we part. Thank you, he says, as if I'd given him something. I cross the road, walk along the pedestrian bridge over the river. It is as brown as ever, with plastic bottles bobbing in the current, plastic bags lining the banks, a mattress poking up in the middle.

A boy is sitting on the bridge. He has a long piece of metal, with several thin spikes extending from it, embedded in his thigh. I can't quite believe what I see. I stop and give him the change I have in my purse, about sixty lek. He puts his hand briefly on his heart, says *zoti te bekofte* (God bless you).

I walk past the Art Gallery in the Rruga Deshmorit, turn right down the street of the Canadian embassy towards my new apartment with the balcony and the view out over the tower blocks and rooftops of Tirana.

8

On Tuesday morning I went with Agron and Mustafa to Zall-Herr commune. This is an area a few kilometres outside Tirana, where we are funding an agriculture project. I was taken on a tour of the greenhouses. The fields are deserted, even the houses seem empty – the farmers have gone to the market in Tirana to sell their vegetables. So you have these silent fields and greenhouses, that deep peaceful silence of hot sun dropping on the land and just the occasional plops of frogs jumping into a murky little pond. Almost all the cucumbers have ripened and have been taken to market. Just a few are left. Mustafa presents me with a prize cucumber and some tomatoes. Agron seems embarrassed by this display of generosity but I am delighted. To go from Zall-Herr village to Pinar village, we drive across the stony bed of a dried-up river.

Once there, I'm led on a tour of Latif Lami's greenhouses – his cucumbers are the biggest I've seen yet. His wife Hamide invites us in and gives us Coca-Cola, followed by Turkish coffee and *raki*. Everyone is so kind, so hospitable and I'm treated as if I'm royalty. This and the *raki* went to my head.

*

Arif is from Azerbaijan and works with Charlie on Water and Sanitation projects. None of our regular drivers were available at the weekend, but Arif claimed he could drive and volunteered to take us over the mountain road to Elbasan, and on to Ohrid in Macedonia. He began by pulling out from the kerb without indicating and Chris said,

Um, Arifi, there's someone coming behind you. Arif's reply was something in the nature of, oh, never mind and he pulled out anyway and of course the other driver did too, being Albanian, and only just missed us. I was sitting in the front seat, feeling nervous.

Arif, slow down, I said, as he hurtled up the Boulevard.

Arif, you've just gone through a red light.

He smiles, ever so slightly, twitches his shoulders almost imperceptibly – for he is not given to dramatic gestures, despite the fact that he confided to me over lunch one day, that he was 'a Lion' – and swings onto the frayed rope of traffic that loops around Scanderbeg Square.

On the outskirts of town, on the Elbasan Road, Arif's attention is distracted by something, he looks over to his left and the car follows his gaze, drifting onto the wrong side of the road.

My nerves have had enough and I request to be let out. The thought of the narrow road to Elbasan, loosely stitched over the mountain peaks like a provisional fringe of bead-work, becomes too much for me. Especially when I think of the sheer drops into deep gullies and the stony crumbling verges with no roadside barriers to break your fall. Remembering too, the sight of rusting metal carcasses, pinned against trees half way down the valley.

I feel a great relief to be walking back down my familiar street, past the Berliner restaurant and the café with the blue gates with *Pepsi* written on them and the poplar trees and the large hole in the road which a car fell into just the other day.

I discovered later that the others had decided not to go on too. I could have driven but I lacked the confidence to go a long way as I've only driven once in Albania. This was when George and I were going to Shkodra to take part in the Emergency Preparedness programme he and Al are running. Part of this training involves teaching people to abseil over rocks and cliffs. We practised going over the pilasters of an abandoned building. The group was being taught 'positive braking' and how to jump down from an overhang rather than climb down a rock face. The danger in this was that if you didn't let yourself drop far enough, you could swing back into the concrete balustrade and hit your face. When it came to my turn I was so concerned with dropping far enough that I forgot to put my right hand behind my back to stop myself falling any further. I just let go completely, but fortunately the brake-man did his job – otherwise I guess I would just have tumbled onto the rock. It was hot of course, but thankfully it clouded over for a while in the afternoon. As it was, the exposed parts of me, shoulders, arms and lower legs, were red with sunburn.

On the way there I asked George if I could drive and I was quite surprised when he had no objections. So I drove some of the way to Shkodra. There is a new piece of road which is straight with no potholes and very little traffic.

This is because there's a very steep and bumpy earthen embankment you have to drive down to get onto it and only Land Cruisers can manage the descent. At one point on this new road you have to make a detour to get around some road works on a bridge. This involves driving along a track then doubling back and going into a rocky dried-up river bed. These vehicles can drive on just about anything. After traversing the stony wasteland you then drive up and through the local rubbish dump before emerging into some delightful fields and tended land that looks like gardens, with fruit trees and old women dressed in black with white scarves on their heads, sitting watching their one cow grazing.

9

The wind in the trees by the lakeside makes a soft ferocious rustling. Wind in the trees too, walking up to the Rruga Deshmorit. There is such sensuality everywhere, but particularly in the rustling trees and the patchy light and shade from vines wound into trellis-work, providing covering, a roof of shifting leaves.

Olga calls me on the phone.

What are you doing today? I'd like to go to the mountains, lie in the grass and sleep.

Yesterday I ran into her, in the Italian supermarket. Almost always, out on the streets, you run into someone you know. Last weekend it was Bardyl. After meeting Bardyl, I went to the Italian store and the owner smiles and nods and follows me around the corner. I call it Italian because I think when I first arrived here Susan called it that, perhaps because many of its products were Italian, or perhaps because they spoke Italian, I'm not sure now, but the owners are clearly Albanian.

I'm looking for salt and sugar and washing up liquid. Sugar is quite easy – *sucre, Zucker*? I ask and he nods and says *sheqer* and hands me a large packet of *Wiener Zucker*. Salt – *sel, sale*? again, is fairly straightforward. I pick up some honey. The owner touches me on the shoulder, keeps his hand there, gestures round the corner to the other aisle. There, he reaches to the back of a shelf and brings out a litre bottle of home-produced honey. He takes off the cap, fills it, insists I taste. It is *very* strong, with a kick in it. I gasp for breath. I wonder what these Albanian bees feed on – something wild and hungry. I nod furiously, but shake my head, repeating *shum mir*, several times, *faleminderit, shum mir*. Albanians shake their heads to mean yes and nod to mean no. However, a small nod can also mean yes.

My mime of washing dishes does not quite work, as he points to washing powder. However I eventually find a whole array of different coloured containers, with pictures of gleaming glasses on them. I think this has to be the right thing and choose *aranchia* scented, vivid red. Albanian cherry jam is next – cheaper than imported jams and with that slightly burnt taste – not burnt, but – what is the word for sugar that's roasted so that it keeps a memory of fire in it? Caramelised, that's it, like crème caramel. Cherry jam caramel.

Then I buy *buke, uje megaz, mozarella fresce*. Meanwhile the owner follows, gesticulates, smiles, touches me on the shoulder. His shop has air conditioning, which tends to make you want to linger, have conversation, pass the time of day.

Yesterday after meeting Olga, I say – I'm not going to run in the park with you, I'm too tired.

I was looking for a pharmacy to get something for the huge red lumps on my arms, from the mosquito bites.

But of course you must come, she says.

But I can't go running like this, I argue feebly.

I can give you clothes, she says. Shorts, T shirt, trainers, everything.

I'm hungry, I say. I was going to buy some bread.

I will get bread. And I have some cheese at home. Mozzarella.

Olga kneads my intent to her will. Like dough, like soft cheese. How can I resist? I follow her back to her apartment.

10

Let me tell you a little bit about this place.

The sound of the frogs at night and in the pond at Zall-Herr, the sound of them dropping into the water. Walking on the dusty path, the air soaked with heat and silence. Just the disappearing sounds of frogs dropping into water. The rich smell of warm hay. The way the sun fell on the fields, stunning the land into complicity. The silence of mid-morning. The ripening tomatoes in the greenhouses.

Driving across a wide stony area, with ridges and gullies of pebbles, rocks, boulders and sandy areas. A dried-up river bed.

A blue Pajero in the middle of the street. One wheel has

fallen into a deep hole.

Further along the Rruga Vaso Pasha, a jutting-out piece of concrete has collapsed. Or been bulldozed, because it's an illegal building.

On the corner of Deshmorit and Bogdane, next to the UNDP building, someone was shot, the other night. A politician, or connected with politics. Or a mafia operation. It's a busy street in the evenings. Two passing pedestrians were also injured. The killer drove off, got away.

The beggar-woman on Rruga Vaso Pasha, with her red shirt and sunburnt skin. The woman who lives on Abdyl Frasheri and is usually sitting – or standing – near the *pasticceria*. She is young, with brownish-fair hair. She never begs. Sometimes she wears an orange shirt. Before the spring came, she would light a small fire on the pavement. I've seen her picking through the garbage bins. She never begs. There is often a beige-haired dog with her. She does not look at anyone, catches nobody's eye. The *pasticceria* is next to the Headquarters of the UN forces – the ones that wear berets blue as a summer sky.

All the trees on Abdyl Frasheri have produced so much greenery that they overflow, hanging down over the pavements, soft shadows, shade-givers. Water sprayed on the pavements turns the dust into a thin layer of mud.

The whine of a tool on steel. The scrape of a chair on ceramic tiles, in the flat above. Melons, dripping with juice. The blaze of sunlight moves slowly across my balcony.

One of the entrances to the apartment block where I now live, is through an old curved archway that comes off the boulevard Bajram Curri. You walk through the yellow-reddish plaster-covered tenements to the new tower block behind them. It's a beige and burnt sienna coloured building. From my balcony on the eighth floor, I look down on the roofs of these older tenements. They have staircases that are open to the sky in between each floor. My apartment block is still unfinished at the bottom. There are pieces of scaffolding and layers of corrugated tin lying around.

The net curtain folds and flaps and shivers in the wind coming through the open window. It drapes itself sensuously against my arm. We're lucky to have the breeze.

The staircase is marble and the banisters are tight, slim, elegant ironwork. They are covered with gritty dust from the construction. Some floors do not have stair lights and the darkness is total. I feel my way cautiously on the steps, fingers light on the grimy banisters. I walk up the stairs if the lift is not working. George once gave me a long lecture on the necessity of knowing how to get out of the lift if it got stuck. Sometimes this happens if there's a power failure. Sometimes it just happens. He told me a story of how he and Al got out of a lift but had to drop down onto the floor below. They had to be careful because if the power had come back on, the lift would have started up again and they could have been crushed. Only much later, after he'd gone, did I remember that he hadn't told me something essential – how do you open the lift doors, a necessary prelude to jumping down, or crawling up.

On the first floor of the Art Gallery, there are large paintings from the socialist realist era. In one, titled *The Partisan*, a young man sits reading a book. A yellow light falls on one side of his face, so I think he must be reading by the light of a camp fire. There is nothing hard in his face, neither angles nor doubt. His face is ashed, like remnants of light, the effects of heat. There is nothing superfluous and nothing held back. The book and the light and his solitude, all have melded into one. He is at the edge of dream. Or the dream has come very close to him, stirring the ash of all that's left behind, all that's been extinguished, in his removal from all earthly desires, into that faint glow, that place where doubt does not exist. Night in the wood, with the breathing of the frogs and the repetitive, sad calling of the djohn-djohn bird and darkness all around except the red glow of the camp fire. I don't know what he is reading, but I am fascinated by the imprint of his thought on his surroundings, so that what you see is the effect of thought and how it has become night and firelight. He thinks night and the movement of yellow light into existence. His thoughts have turned into light.

Driving over the railway at the level crossing, I automatically look both ways. A man walks along the track, with his flock of sheep, heads lowered, bells sounding, like the noise of wind turning corners or side-stepping boulders or leaning against the path at the edge of the hill. Wind tracks. That's what stayed in the memory, the sunlight and the hill slopes of the south. The sound of goat bells and sheep bells. The sound of water drifting round a shore and heading back to sea. The sound of flowers opening and closing. The sound of sunlight slipping on the steep hillsides, coming to rest, and walking unsteadily back up the slope to the top. The sound of the earth breathing, waking up and drifting back to sleep again. The sound of cowbells. The smell of jasmine, waking you in early morning.

11

Olga calls me.

Can I sleep on your sofa for a couple of nights? You see, I have decided to leave Jean-Paul.

Of course, I say.

When she comes round in the evening, her face is sombre.

I'm going to look for my own apartment, she says. I could have stayed at Chris's flat, he has a spare room, but I know Jean-Paul would think that I had left him for Chris, if I stayed there. Jean-Paul said, the first time he saw Chris, that he was the one person he would not want me to spend time alone with.

While Chris was not the only person whose company Olga sought out, they were often together. Sometimes they went running in the park. Usually there were other people there as well. I'd even gone myself, a couple of times. Jean-Paul seemed to be absent from these excursions. Perhaps he didn't like to go running.

A few days later Olga moved into an apartment near the top of Abdyl Frasheri, close to the Boulevard. The outside of the building is grey stained concrete, but inside it is wood-panelled, the floor laid with delicate varnished parquet which creaks as you walk over it. It is a ground floor apartment with its own little garden, big enough for a table and a few chairs, sheltered from the street by a dense and high hedge. Olga seems to be happy with her new home. She moved her possessions bit by bit. She spent a lot of time on the phone to Jean-Paul.

He keeps asking me to go back with him, but I cannot go back, she said.

She often made arrangements to see him though, when he felt lonely and missed her and wanted to talk to her.

I feel guilty sometimes, she said, but what can I do? For a long time, I've not been happy with him. But I feel sad for him, yes. He is lonely, he has not really made friends here.

Just after Olga moved into her new apartment, I had a beer with Chris one evening after work. He told me he had split up with his girlfriend.

It had been difficult for some time, he said. She wanted me to fly over to London every other weekend and that's not really possible in this kind of work. You don't always get weekends off, as you know. But it came to a head when she asked me if I was really committed to the relationship and I didn't feel I could honestly say yes to that.

I asked him how he felt about it.

I'm sad in a way obviously, but it's also a bit of a relief. It's just too difficult to keep going back to London as often as she'd like me to.

We were sitting in the garden outside Ravena's. The sky was turning a deep pink and evening was settling in, basking in the sunset like a scroll of uncurled light.

And Olga? I asked him.

I don't know. She is wonderful, oh yes, but I don't know if it could possibly work between us.

But something was at work and Chris and Olga seemed to be arranging their lives to allow space for that possibility, even while they found other reasons for their actions, even while they might deny to others and even to themselves, that the reason for their choices had anything to do with each other. Some energy was at work, making deft arrangements. Chris and Olga no more controlled this energy than they did the sunrise. Yet it manipulated them just as the sunrise tinkers with our feelings, our reactions, our motives and our desires. We can hardly call them 'ours' yet we sometimes made claims to ownership and to control, because that is often what we like to think. That the rational mind is in control. Meanwhile the sun beats down and the tides shift the sea's tongue to lick the sand. And the evening light turns crimson as Chris and I part outside Ravena's and I walk back along Vaso Pasha and turn right under the archway.

12

National boundaries in the Balkans have a fluctuating malleable quality. While an area in northern Greece was once part of Albania, the southern part of Albania was once known as Northern Epiros. In southern Albania there is still a sizeable minority of ethnic Greeks. I came to realise that national and ethnic boundaries are not at all the same thing. Ethnic Albanians living in Macedonia for example, with Macedonian passports, consider themselves Albanian. Ethnic Greeks living in Albania still think of themselves as Greek. Ethnicity becomes the strongest link and when tensions arise, divisions show up along ethnic fault-lines, rather than national boundaries, which were often imposed by some outside power anyway.

In the troubles of 1997, when the Pyramid schemes in Albania collapsed, and so many people lost all their money and sometimes their homes, there was rioting and looting, particularly of supplies of arms. With a large part of the population now armed, law and order collapsed.

Many ethnic Greeks, fearing for their lives, abandoned their homes and crossed the border into Greece.

Many houses in the village of Dhermis are still empty. Untended vines, olive trees and general vegetation trail across buildings and paint-peeled doors, fastened by rusting padlocks. There is a deserted feel to these houses and the stretching vegetation leans across them, nimble and luxuriant under the hot sun. These abandoned properties clearly belong to others, but even for those who are still living here, there are huge problems with land ownership throughout Albania. This has resulted from land claimed by the government during the communist regime, being claimed back by the previous owners or their descendants and there are often conflicting claims. And since 1997, with much of the population now possessing arms, the threat of violence has become a powerful manipulative tool for settling disputes. I witnessed a graphic demonstration of this in Dhermis.

It was our second visit to this tiny coastal resort by the Ionian Sea. On our first visit, at Easter, it had been deserted. The coastline, the ocean, the restaurant which opened for us when we arrived late in the evening, the scent of jasmine and orange blossom, all had been ours alone. But now, in the summer season, the two hotels were full of visitors, there was a choice of restaurants and cafés and the beach, while not exactly as crowded as popular Mediterranean tourist resorts and sun traps, was certainly populated.

Except in the early morning, when I had the hotel's private beach to myself. It was made up of pebbles, all smooth and rounded, some very small, like compact little sea-seeds, some quite large. All white, with tinges of violet. The sea was utterly transparent and palest turquoise.

During the week-end I spent a lot of time in the sea. It was full of light. The surface was covered in points of reflected sunlight, dazzling and winking and constantly changing. And when I put my head underwater, there on the pale and creamy stones and sand were the moving patterns of lights that danced on the surface, dancing too on the seabed. I swam, floated, basked and with a snorkel, put my head under the surface and watched the play of light. I am not a good or adventurous swimmer, it was the intimate sensuality of the warm water and the way it held me, its currents shifting underneath me and washing over my skin, cooling the fierceness of the sun's heat, that kept drawing me back into the water.

On Sunday morning before going to the beach I was sitting outside the hotel beneath the shade of a tree, about to have breakfast, when a van pulled up in front of the building, just a few metres away from me. My omelette had just arrived on the table. Several men got out of the van, two of them carrying Kalashnikovs.

They started shouting and the people who run the hotel came out and there was more shouting and gesticulating, some loud altercations and a bit of pushing and shoving. I noticed that the people who had been sitting at the other tables had disappeared. I watched this going on just a few metres away and deliberated what to do but as there did not seem to be any real danger I decided to eat my omelette anyway. The little waiter came over and said don't be afraid and I thought that was very kind of him so I told him I wasn't – which was true, as it was clear that all this had nothing to do with me. Eventually all the men, including the ones with guns, piled back into the van, and it turned around and headed back down the road, watched by the hotel staff. The hotel manager came over to me and apologised. He explained that the problem was over a land dispute, but had nothing to do with their hotel, it concerned the one further down the road, built on someone else's land. Whether it did or not, the Kalashnikov-filled van did not stop there, but turned the corner out of sight, and presumably headed back up the steep hill leading to the village.

*

In the afternoon I walk up the steep hill lined with terraces of olive trees to the village of Dhermis. The cicadas shimmer the air, rattle it like hundreds of miniature maracas. The air drums lightly. A cowbell sounds, falls silent, sounds again.

I visit the little Orthodox Church just off the road, that we saw the first time we came to Dhermis. Many of the frescos are complete but parts of some of them have been stained or smudged with damp. There is clearly a restoration project going on. The ceiling is wooden and painted with flaking images. There is a single chair in the middle, with a candle stub on it. It is cool inside the church and the sunlight is a bright flare in the doorway. I sit for a while on the chair. Some cool presence comes up behind me, curls round me, lifts me up. A soaring peace.

In the evening Chris, Olga and I take a paddle boat out in the water and watch the sun go down. The sea turns deep shades of bluish purple and indigo, with flecks and fragments of yellow orange and red from the sun's light, like shards from broken stained glass windows scattered on the sea surface. I remember what Dhermis was like in April, when there were no other tourists and the jasmine blossom was out. Just this layer of rustling sound the sea washed up.

On the drive back to Tirana we sing songs, with Dave, who was obviously some court jester in a past life, cracking jokes all the time. When we get back to the dusty city, there is a murky yellow fingernail moon low in the sky.

13

Today being the 4th July, we have an official holiday as all true Americans should and those of us not American by birth are so by default, being employed by an American company. However having said that, some of us took the day off yesterday instead to make the weekend longer. So I am working today but at home which allows greater flexibility and more cups of tea, but has the disadvantage of no fan and when you're sitting in front of the Devil's Oven (waves of heat wafting in from outside) thoughts turn to the idea of a fan the way thirsty people's thoughts turn to water. The mind becomes all elbows, obsessively nudging the thought into your consciousness, a persistent distraction.

The streets are piled with huge watermelons. They are dark-green like dim interiors, with ice-green stripes of light falling on them. There are cantaloupe melons as well, their insides a dusky orange, tinged with green near the rind, and dripping with sweetness. Corn on the cob is roasted over small grilles. There's a heatwave rolling over the Balkans – hot winds blowing up from the Sahara desert, so they say. Temperatures are well into the forties – this is high, even for here. I buy a bikini for 2,000 lek (about £10) in one of the chichi little basement shops on the street that leads to the pedestrian bridge over the river. It's Saturday afternoon and we go to the swimming pool which is unbelievably crowded. There's a lot of shouting laughter and splashing as young Albanian men push each other into the water. There's barely room to swim, but I shuffle up and down the length of the pool. The water is tepid rather than cool, and dries quickly on your skin in the baking, unmoving air.

*

Matt announced yesterday that he's leaving. He originally came to this country as a journalist during the crisis of 1999 and he wants to return to that work, in Kosova. While we were lounging by the swimming pool at the week-end, Matt headed for Kukës, a town in the north east of Albania, with a reputation for lawlessness and banditry. According to Matt, he had taken the Land Cruiser to a car wash and was waiting for his turn, the vehicle just a few metres in front of him. Two men with guns appeared and started shooting at the car. Matt jumped up, ran into the nearest field and dove to the ground, spraining his wrist as he did so. He found out later that the men with guns had some kind of grievance against the car-wash people and just picked on the Land Cruiser because it happened to be there. So he came back from Kukës with his arm in plaster and a sling, and a Jeep with two shot tyres and a crop of bullet holes in the windscreen.

14

The problem with Australians is that they are the victims of Vegemite Francesco said, as we walked along the Rruga Sami Frasheri towards the bridge. When I asked him if he spoke French he said *Je parle français comme une vache espagnol.*

S'il te plaît?

Très mal.

In the street today, three people had already spoken to me or asked me something. I must really be looking like an *echt* Albanian these days. One was an older man – because I recognised Rruga Kavaje in his question, I was actually able to help him. He spoke English – one of these gentle, courteous older men, with such kind eyes and a smile – do you know the kind of smile I mean? – such history in that smile – a mixture of delight, pain and a touch of longing. The sadness of the past mixing with relief and delight at the past's disappearance. I would have loved to sit down and talk to him, but I was already late for work.

After work I went to the supermarket just up from the Paradise Restaurant, on the Rruga Myslym Shyri. It was empty as usual. Apart from one other person, who spoke to me as I drifted past the cereal counter. I smiled politely, made my usual response – *me fall, nuk flas Shqip* (I'm sorry, I don't speak Albanian). He looked at me and said something else in English.

I know you're not Albanian, I was just wondering about this cereal. Do you think I should get this? Is this OK? I never buy this stuff.

He was clutching a packet of cornflakes in his hand. His English was very good, but accented.

I'm not Albanian, I'm Italian, he said and my daughter's coming tomorrow and I know she likes cereal, but there are so many kinds, I don't know –

Personally I like the *croccante*, I say, but it depends – how old is your daughter?

I was thinking of the sweet things and funny shapes that young children often like.

She's twenty-four, he said.

I giggled.

Oh well – why not get her some of this – pointing to a packet called *Perfetto* or *perfettamente* or something similar, with raisins and bits of dried fruit in it as well.

Healthy kind of stuff – that will impress her.

Impress her? he said. OK I'll take that as well.

And that is how I met Francesco, 'Superior Inspector' as his card says, with MAPE, the Western European Union.

*

After our first meeting in the supermarket in Rruga Myslym Shyri, Francesco emails me. Would I like to meet up on Wednesday evening, at the café in front of the supermarket? Yes, I reply. His apartment is just opposite and he invites me up. His living room is crammed with books and the walls are lined with his drawings and paintings.

Francesco comes through from the kitchen and hands me a cold beer. He opens a file on his computer, shows me images of some of his other paintings.

I will have an exhibition in Rome when I go back, he says. But I have not made so many paintings this year. I have been six years here in Albania. I think I would like to live somewhere else – maybe Africa.

He shows me a trick. He takes a piece of foil, rolls it

into a ball. He holds it in his hand for a few moments. Then puts it in my hand. It is very hot, almost burning my palm. He shrugs it off. It's just something I can do – it's not important.

Then he says he has this pasta he needs to use up – he's going back to Italy in a few days – would I like some? And tomato salad? I say yes.

While Francesco is in the kitchen, I look at the drawings on the walls. The faces and the *natures mortes* have detail shade and subtlety that seem to draw on a perception beyond the visual range. He makes the real thing look like cast-offs, careless first attempts, abandoned imperfect practices, scrawled exercises. His da Vinci-esque shaded pencil detail reveals layers of subtle perception that daylight and the hurried eye, riffling through the contents of vision to some other, as yet undiscovered, some future goal, will always fail to see. These drawings arrest time, with their focus on the enormity of the present moment.

I pause, in the crowded little room, full of books, papers, paintings. I look out of the window. The street below is a narrow dusty path. The apartment block opposite is just a few metres away. This is what art is I think, this ability to vanish time, to disappear the weight of it, to melt its nagging voices, like a background Greek chorus, which must be constantly appeased in a variety of ways, to prevent the emergence of the Eumenides, bursting through the stage doors of our consciousness, threatening to tear us limb from limb.

We're no different from the ancient Romans I think, we make propitiatory gestures all the time, to keep the vengeance of the gods at bay. The difference is that we don't acknowledge gods and we often do not recognise what it is we do. We might admit to awareness of a vague angst lurking at our mind's frontiers, but we don't have to let it in, because we think its home is in some other country and not ours. Meanwhile, we move faster, faster, what we have to do increases and the days shrink alarmingly and so there is 'no time' to be fully in the present moment.

In the apartment off Myslym Shyri, I see how art can ease us into the present, removing the fearful mutterings of the Eumenides at one stroke – if we can allow ourselves that pause and presence and trust that the artist did, when he created it.

15

Florian comes with me to the Kalaje restaurant where Matt's leaving party is being held. Matt is looking well, despite his arm still in plaster and a sling, from his Kukës adventure. Someone gives him a present of a white fez, traditional headgear for Northern Albanians. The evening is full of conversation and laughter, music and dancing, wine and *raki*. Later, when I say I'm going home, Florian leaves with me, and we walk back down the Boulevard, along Bajram Curri and turn left along the silent, deserted Rruga Vaso Pasha.

*

It began to rain. Standing up on the steps outside the Opera in Scanderbeg Square, I looked out over the huge circle of waltzing cars on a shiny grey cobbled rink.

The muezzin had begun the call to prayer as I walked

past the Ethem Bey mosque – a slow, low, seductive chant – Allah, Allah. It coils around me and my steps slow and I feel dizzy. It lures, it tugs and I want nothing more than this, I want to become this chant, I want to become only this, always. It glides around my spine, reaching to my feet, massaging my solar plexus, rushing up to the corpus callosum, the fiery, sparking hat of enlightenment.

I turn around. I cannot walk away from it. I go up the steps outside the Opera. Look over towards the statue of Scanderbeg on his horse, and the trees behind him. These trees are some variety of pine, with long wavy arms that drift downwards, languid, supplicant. A flag uncurls beside the statue – the red flag with the black double-headed eagle, the red dulled in places, bleached from the sun, stained from the exhaust fumes and limp from the rain.

I saw them all as banners – statue, trees and flag, and I saw through the emblems to what lies behind. Maybe it was the rain that slid open the doors, the unlocking properties of rain – but I saw them as the veil that this world is and what lies behind it. All with the low chant carried by the loudspeakers across the wide square. It reached out with its eagle claws of perception and grabbed my heart and I surrendered on the steps of Scanderbeg Square, I gave in, as the light rain fell all around me.

*

We are walking along Vaso Pasha, Florian and I. It's about 2 in the morning and the moon is almost full. The street is deserted and utterly silent. Florian puts out his elbow and takes my hand to put through his arm.

In the silent street there is just the rhythmic clink of my anklet and the pat, crunch of his shoes on the road, clink, clip clip, clink, clip clip and the pale, smudgy lunar shadows and the dark trees, evasive and sheltering.

We go through the dark alley leading into the yard behind, and the entrance to my apartment block. I fiddle with the keys, trying to see which is the one for the outside door, the big metal door that creaks like a door in a horror movie and slams shut like the door exiling Eve and Adam from the garden.

What number are you, he asks, looking at the names on the buzzers, so I'll know which one to press, if I come by –

Twenty-nine, I say, squinting at the keys.

Give them to me, let me try –

But one of them fits –

Just try them, he says, takes them from me and bends over to put a key in the lock, which is placed awkwardly low down on the sheet of grey metal.

The door creaks open, the only sound, or so it seems, in the whole of the silent, sleeping city.

*

The rain gets heavier as I leave Scanderbeg Square, walk along the Boulevard, cross over and head down the Bulevardi Zhane d'Arc. The pedestrian bridge to the Rruga Durresit has a coating of water on it. A few people stand under trees. I pass the French patisserie that sells *buke francesi,* and the music shop, and turn down the Canadian Embassy street. Rubbish has overflowed from the garbage bins, mixes with the rainwater and the gravel of the broken-up pavements to form a brownish mush, which in places turns into fast-flowing rivulets.

The rain has soaked through my T-shirt and trousers and my heart has been ambushed and flicked open like a knife.

Gods of Roads and Open Doorways

...If the nut
of the mystery can't be held,
at least let me touch the shell
Rumi

1

The weather has broken. Just like the sounds of breaking glass that come through the window, there are pieces of it flying all around, broken bits of weather wafting and banking and surging like waves through the air and round about Dajti mountain, all cloud-covered and looming, all shoulder-shrugging and moody, fiercely wrapping itself in dark-grey, banks and strips of it, layers of different varieties of grey, a dream of monochrome, a fever of shades.

The outside of my apartment block is painted in two different colours – cream and that difficult-to-define shade that hovers between brown and purple – terracotta soaked in vinegar and sprinkled with plum juice. From my window I can see other candy-coloured apartment blocks

– puce-pink and white, creamy with a hint of salmon pink and white, blue and white and two-tone green, apple and a more bluish-green shade. The older buildings have more traditional colours – yellow plaster and orange-red tiles.

The rain started as a refreshing drizzle then turned into a serious race on the part of raindrops to see who could reach the ground first. Rain quickly turns into little rivers in Tirana, puddles and potholes fill up fast and water spreads out, covering half the street in places and almost totally covering the pedestrian bridge that leads to the Rruga Durresit. You watch the ground as you walk to avoid stepping in large puddles or even larger uncovered manholes, avoiding too the odd bit of detritus sailing by on a new-found watery purpose, searching for the direction of the sea.

It is cold. I have had to put on a long-sleeved shirt. I was uptown having breakfast in the Stefan Centre when it began to rain. The Stefan Centre serves the most delicious apple pancakes with butter and honey. You can also get a bottomless cup of coffee for a mere 70 lek (35p). Having breakfast is not something I normally do, but I was persuaded by Donika from the Elbasan office, who comes and sleeps on the living-room sofa from time to time, if she needs somewhere to stay in Tirana. So wonderful was this feast, that Saturday morning pancakes could become a tradition.

Friday night was Dave's leaving party and a gaping hole is left in all of our hearts, with the departure of the court jester. Who will make us laugh now, when tempers fray and Tourette syndrome rears its unexpected head in the office? Who will dig out Band-Aids from a tiny box buried underneath a heap of files and a much larger box with 'condoms – for office use only' written on it? Who will give us jabs for tetanus, rabies, cholera-typhoid, polio, and hepatitis B? And, most importantly, who will mix cheerful cocktails of fruit juice, Ponç (orange-flavoured liqueur) and Fernet, (a heady mixture that tastes like cough medicine and Germolene) vodka, and special Lord Bajron champagne? Since there is clearly no-one to take his place we are planning to form a pressure group called SOBS (Society of Bereaved friendS) to try to get him back here on one pretext or another, as soon as possible.

As I write, the clouds are sliding out of our chunk of Adriatic-coastline sky, and a pleasant blue is spreading in the wake of grey.

*

On a trip to Elbasan I noticed a new wall mosaic, one I had not seen before. On the road that curls down into the valley, one side has been shored up with stones, and the mosaic is embedded in this embankment. It depicts a heroic group, full of determination and patriotic fervour. This is a familiar theme but this one is more unusual in that all the group are women, pushing forward guns. Guns are such ubiquitous and potent symbols here. True, there's a statue in Tirana park of a woman giving water to a soldier, and another in Lushnija of a woman holding aloft a sheaf of corn, with the same pose of defiant and heroic success – but mainly it's guns.

The roadside stalls selling apples, bananas, olive oil, have makeshift shelters and their coverings are of branches and bracken, all the dried leaves turned russet now. Part of the road to Elbasan runs along the top of the mountain, a knife-edge, with valleys falling away on either side.

The factory leaks an orange coloured smoke. We drive

to the Hotilishti school near the Macedonian border, to discuss the summer camps with teachers and parents. On the way back we pass through Librazhd with its poise and sense of harmony and its wide and leafy tree-lined streets. Its sense of cultivated arboreal opulence contrasts vividly with the half-demolished, half-reconstructed clutter, abandoned buildings half pulled down and machinery that's left to rust, that you find in other parts of Albania.

2

On Monday evening I drove up to Shkodra with George. The evening light lay soft on the hills. The bridge on the new stretch of road is almost completed but we still had to drive around it, through the stony river bed which, because of the heavy rains at the weekend, had gone back to being a river. In the evening Al, George, Mark and I strolled through the deserted streets of Shkodra. The silence was carpeted by the liquid sound of frogs. This was followed by the call to prayer, a low sound reverberating through the empty streets. A couple of dogs howled in the distance while the full moon watched over us.

I slept in the upstairs room in the office. The balcony off this room is the same one where I watched the woman on the opposite balcony, with her huge tub of flour. That was February and already the sun had warmth in it. Now it's July and the night air is thick with heat.

We were in Shkodra to take part in a Navigation Exercise. George and Al are ex-military and the plan for the day was for them to lead a group of Albanian students in a Search and Rescue Exercise. The students would be taught the skills of map and co-ordinate reading, and the use of a compass. The exercise was a mock scenario of a downed aircraft and the students' task would be to find the position of the aircraft and the survivors.

Our day started early, at 5.30, to avoid the worst of the heat in the afternoon. The sun had risen by the time we had picked everyone up, and we drove out of Shkodra through an area where garbage was piled high on either side of the road and was probably the rubbish dump for the whole town. After we left that behind we turned off the main road and headed for the hills. Early morning sunlight in a cloudless sky of deep blue, with soft green hills rising in the distance. This was a world away from city life, a world that seemed quite untouched by humanity, as if no humans had ever been there before. A secret, verdant valley.

And once we'd climbed the first hill the land fell away in front of us, with a view out over the lake and nearby hills, crested with sunlight and softened with slight haze. I took pictures and interviewed some of the participants, as I would be writing an article about the exercise. Then I left the others to their maps and compasses and took a short-cut down to the lake, where we would all meet up afterwards.

The descent was very steep and the hillside had rough patches of loose stones and scree, intermixed with areas of thick brambles and thorn bushes. I slipped and fell over a couple of times and was very glad there was no one there to see me. I arrived at the lakeside shaken, bruised and scratched, but with a secret sense of accomplishment.

Bardyl was there, with two small boys who had joined him. Although both of them stared at me, the way these children do, the older one was particularly beautiful, with an open and vulnerable expression. Bardyl pointed out that he'd had an accident with a grenade a few years ago during the troubles, and had lost his left hand. I hadn't even noticed until he mentioned it, I'd been so captivated with his face.

So I sat next to Bardyl in the small area of shade beneath the tree, close to the stones by the lake-shore and we talked a little and the boy with the beautiful, open face stared at me. Besnik the driver arrived and was soon followed by the others who made their way down the hill by a less direct route than the one I had taken, and I helped gather wood for the barbecue. Potatoes, fish and meat were cooked and afterwards we swam in the murky water of the lake to cool off.

Coming back from Shkodra in the evening, George drove through the archway off Rruga Bajram Curri to go to my apartment building. The archway is lined with big garbage bins which of course have spilled over, leaving rubbish piled in heaps around them. On the other side of the archway there are also mounds of garbage, bits of tiles and flattened tin cans, cardboard boxes and pieces of twisted and discarded metal and broken glass and general debris. Mark is new here and it was the first time he had seen this alley. He said in astonishment – is this where you live? It's like Beirut. I was quite offended. I've got so used to this I don't see it as anything out of the ordinary. George replied no, it's a really nice apartment. He too, I think, just does not see the rubble and litter any more. Besides, this is the area known as The Blok, the select part of town!

On Saturday evening Simon called and we went for a walk in the park and a wander through the streets of

Tirana. We walked past the pyramid and up to Scanderbeg Square, eating a *sufflaq* on the way, walking through the dark street past the post office where there are lots of trees and no lights at all. From these peaceful shadows we continued down the street with the shops in the basements that sell *kepuçe* and fashionable Italian clothes, and on towards the Bulevardi Zhane d'Arc and the little pedestrian bridge over to the Rruga Deshmorit, turning right down Bajram Curri, past the café Lord Bajron, and the arched entrance to my apartment block.

This morning I hear little clip clop sounds and I look over the balcony and there's a horse walking around the area below, pulling a cart. It pulls up in front of the pile of rubbish and the driver gets out and searches among the rubble. He picks up a couple of pieces of twisted metal and puts them in the cart to join the other things he's got in there.

3

I cross the road bridge over the canal, turn left up Rruga Bajram Curri, this familiar street, with the *akullore* shop and the shop that plays loud music and another small shop on the corner, crowded inside, with a refrigerator outside, with tubs of ice-cream in it. Turn right there, along the Berliner restaurant street or the Banka Kombetare street.

I was up in a different part of town, past the clock-tower off Scanderbeg Square and it reminded me of how I felt when I first came here, when everything was strange, the streets, the people and the way they walked and looked at you and the sound of the language. But when you get to know certain streets and a certain area, when you get used to a place and the sound of a language, your relationship with it becomes entirely different. Some phrases I hear I now understand – *nu ka dit, mijdas, na rego, faleminderit, mirupafshim, mir dita, shum mir* –

And the familiarity of it forms something around you, something you wear, like clothes, close to your skin and I wear these streets and the shady trees, I wear the broken pavements and the smooth new hexagonal paving stones, I wear the big glass building on the left-hand side of Bajram Curri, and it reflects the old, yellow, crumbly-plaster buildings opposite, with their Italianate metal grilles over balconies, their shutters and slanted, faded canopies jutting out from the windows, over balconies –

Cherries have disappeared from the fruit-vendors stalls but there are still heaped piles of streaky-green watermelons, still nectarines and peaches and today I saw the first bunches of black grapes.

The corn-roasters sit on upturned wooden boxes on street-corners. Their makeshift barbecues are small tin trays, filled with ashy charcoal. Smells of roasting corn drift across the pavement as you walk past.

I wear these streets like a cape thrown across my shoulders, so close to me they are protective and beloved and sewn into my skin as securely as the sunlight has altered its shade to beige, as familiar as the damp sweat that sticks your clothes to your skin and as welcome as the slight breeze that shuffles up between your skin and your clothes, eddies of some imagined cool water splashing on your head and trickling down your arms. Summer bakes the air and runs over your limbs like a memory of Eden, whipped-cream water-melon memory, pink fruit and black seeds you spit out, juice running down your chin.

These streets have become part of my geography, worn into my skin like steps. Anyone touching me could walk through my memories and feel the rubble and the broken pavements and the dust and the flagstones smooth as silk beneath their toes.

4

On Sunday morning I went to the gypsy market. It's located between Rruga Myslym Shyri and Rruga Bajram Curri on an area of waste land. There you find all the clothes that people have donated to refugees, which never quite reached them, all spread out, and selling for 100 lek a piece (about $1). It was like an open air charity shop or jumble sale. It was crowded, colourful and noisy. All the vendors were shouting – the gist of it I think was that everything cost only 100 lek. I bought a blue cotton dress and a pair of baggy shorts. Some of the Roma children were playing their instruments – a reedy clarinet. If there had been queues I would have been lost – I have not yet mastered the art of pushing in front of everybody that Albanians are so good at.

In the post office for example, valuing personal space, I stand back a bit from the person being served. Inevitably, one or more people walk in front of me and lean on the counter. I find this so frustrating I've taken to only going to the post office very early in the morning or late in the evening or on Sundays when it's not so busy, to avoid this cultural torture. There is only one post office in Tirana and no post boxes that I can see. In fact I've no idea how people get mail delivered here, unless you have a post office box, as we do at work. For there are no letter boxes on doors, though I have seen some red Albpost vans around. There is nowhere else you can buy stamps either, so posting letters is a carefully planned exercise.

Outside the post office are lots of people trying to sell you phone cards and on the corner are crowds of men offering to change money for you. Money changing on the street is quite legal and acceptable and you get a better rate than the bank, which is a very lengthy and tedious process. I've only been to a bank once, accompanied by Anxhela from the Finance Office who knew what she was doing, but even so it took a long time and various forms had to be filled in. We also had to wait outside as there were a lot of policemen with guns there, probably waiting to escort someone in or out.

Getting past the money-changers takes time and effort as you have to keep saying *jo faleminderit* (no thank you) to everyone who pushes a bunch of lek in your face. You also have to remember (and I frequently forget) that to shake your head means yes, while to nod means no.

A few of us went to the cinema to see *Mission Impossible Two*. Trying to get served to buy a can of EVI Limon beforehand was just as impossible as anything Tom Cruise tried to do, with hordes of people shoving in front of you and shouting, so I got Ylli to do it for me. The film was a wonderful piece of escapism, but I couldn't look at the bits where he was hanging from a cliff thousands of miles up, just by his finger-ends, I got vertigo.

5

I keep waking up really early in the morning. I hear the barking of dogs and the whining of mosquitoes. The first muezzin call comes before dawn while the morning is still dark and the city has not yet woken up. Sound carries easily in the darkness and the low chant throws a veil of magic over the morning, somewhere between dream and wakefulness. Soon after that the sound of a passing truck in the dark streets makes me think of travel. I want to be on the move again.

This morning is hung between pink flecks of cloud, and there's a moon that's growing crumply at the edge, wilting like a dry and curling leaf. The high-pitched curve of swifts. The pre-dawn call to prayer rolls through the dark streets, low in the sky. I go for these high places always – the noon call of the muezzin across the wet square, the pine trees by the Scanderbeg statue, shivering in the rain.

This is a country that clings to heroism like a glove. The psyche of this country, like the land, is full of cliffs, ravines and precipices. Honour is the path you walk. The coastal strip opens from the high ridges and mountain passes, like a flower that reveals what the mountains hid. It paints it and then wilts and disappears.

For all the space, there is a sense of being folded and cocooned in rock. The mind is terraced, like a vineyard, with beliefs, running as deep as the valley floor. They lie in gorges, painted on rock walls, reminding you of feelings that do not belong to you. You are a slip of their tongue, an incidental seed arriving on damp soil. You inhale only a flicker of this feeling and it removes all solid ground. After that, there is the sea – roped and gemmed with light, pale green and salty. Holding you up, like time. Swallowing you, like time. There is that pull, that magnetism and whether you go with it or resist, whether you deny it, rush inside it, revere it or cajole it, it is there. It may speak to you or it may stay silent. What god is tracking me?

To not desperately desire a certain outcome – there's a thing. To be accepting of either outcome – yes or no. To not cling with feverish nails to what you want so much to be the future. To remain open to the possibilities – of this or that. To not *need* it to be one thing or the other. What god is that? The god of roads or open doorways? Or the god that shows you a clear pathway to your heart? For the heart does not choose this and reject that. The heart embraces and in this way, heals the mind's divisions.

The salt god, that floats you on the water. The god that tends the garden, sweeping aside dead leaves and branches. He asks no questions. He is very quiet. He looks at you as you walk through the entrance. He notes the patterns that the sea has made on you, the little ridges and indentations, the colours of the sky at dawn. With the marks of the sea's fingers on you, he leaves you free to wander in this garden. You move closer to him, watch the muscles in his shoulders. He hands you a brush. And you begin to sweep.

6

The temperature is rising again. Nothing much happens on the streets of Tirana on Sunday afternoons. Some people are working on a building site, pouring concrete into foundations. On a much smaller project, near Rob's apartment, two others are lining up steps leading to a couple of small shops, and mixing concrete to make new ones. Rob is an Australian engineer working for the UN and he tells me that the old steps were bulldozed a couple of days ago.

And the kiosk just across the street was completely broken up, he says, this happens fairly frequently, as people build or erect things without getting the proper permission – or perhaps not paying the right amount of money – then the 'building police' come along and bulldoze the buildings.

I notice that the bulldozed buildings are usually quite small, but bigger, flashier ones, strangely enough, go unscathed, even when the frontage of their building extends out onto the pavement further than the permissible dimensions.

Back at work after my mysterious illness (which might have been due to lack of salt) and not being able to eat anything much except fruit, I took to going out at lunch time and buying lots of it – pears, nectarines, grapes, figs, melon. People would come by my office and have some fruit, particularly Sameh, the new Health Officer, who's replaced Dave. He could be relied on to polish off half a kilo. He's even taken to suggesting what varieties of fruit I should get the next day. However, it's very handy to have a doctor available all the time to make quick diagnoses and reassure you. When I was ill he took my pulse and told me to drink lots of water. When I told him I felt faint he thought about this for a minute and then said – 'faint?' (he is Egyptian and has an endearing way of speaking that makes his voice go up at the end as if he is constantly questioning everything).

You can feel faint if you have dysentery, he said.

Thanks Sameh, I replied.

Yesterday a few of us went to the gorge, which is part way up Dajti mountain, where the river runs between rocks and forms a deep pool before continuing. This road isn't used much, and the cliffs and small mountains have a sense of peace to them. On the way we notice a few massive containers, in semi-camouflage colours, tucked into the mountainside. These are apparently empty now, but were used to store petrol in the communist times. Just beyond them are military buildings, deserted now, some of them half ruined. Two or three tanks are still there, parked behind some of the buildings. A donkey walks slowly along the road, on its own, piled with a green load of grass so high you can barely see its head poking out. Every so often, it moves its neck slightly and takes a mouthful of grass. A couple of people, presumably the donkey's owners, are standing by the roadside, holding big scythes.

The water was refreshing, but very cold. While I was warming up on the rocks afterwards, I noticed some little frogs floating in the water. Their noses (if frogs have noses) were just touching the water surface, and they were quite motionless, suspended in the water, basking in the warmth from the sun.

I've applied for my leave days this week. I'm taking the ferry from Durres and going to visit Italy.

7

Andi drives me to Durres to catch the ferry to Bari. We don't talk much. He speaks Italian. I understand what he says, but lack the vocabulary to answer him. We drive along the dusty road, overtaking when we can. We pass carts and loaded donkeys. At one point he says my name as if tasting it, like a pale pink ice of watermelon, or a gulp of wine going down your throat.

In the queue to embark the policeman told me to go and get my passport stamped. I waited in front of the wrong booth, but the man there, all dark-eyed and dark-skinned and hesitant English, told me I had to go to the building behind. I found a policeman standing at the door, so presented him with my passport which he took and got stamped, which meant I didn't have to wait in the long queue.

I return to the queue to embark. The policeman smiles with satisfaction at the stamp, but the next official, looking at my ticket, nods his head, a bad sign. I have to go back to the office next to the Dogana to get the boarding pass. It's hot, sweat gathers on my under lip and between my breasts. The boarding pass secured, I can finally make my way into the crowded boat. I manage to find a hard plastic seat in front of a table and get out my notebook.

The ferry skips across the Adriatic like a crazy frog. The surface is calm – the horizon is hazy. The sea looks as though a god has sighed across its surface – misted, kissed.

I think you are writing something beautiful, says the young man opposite me as I pause and gaze out of the window. He tells me he's Albanian, from Macedonia, and now lives in Belgium. I go out to the back with him to have a cigarette. This ferry is not like the spacious ones I'm used to, but more like a bus that floats or rather skips over the water. *La Vikinga* has a central area, where you sit. And that's it. There are toilets at the back. Next to them there are a few steps up to the deck, but you're not allowed on deck. This area with steps however, is where the Albanians stand and smoke. When I return to my seat I doze off a couple of times, tired from last night's wine and lack of sleep.

On arrival in Bari we stand in line to go through customs. An Italian policeman has a German shepherd dog on a lead, shouts at people who try to cut past the queue and snaps his fingers when it's time for the next two people to move forward to have their passports examined. This is an operation that can take some time. Passports are scrutinised, slowly and thoroughly. Questions are asked, sometimes there are lengthy verbal exchanges, accompanied by more passport page flicking. Eventually, documents are handed back, slowly, reluctantly. It's as if the immigration officials are hoping that if they slow things down enough, all the people from the boat will give up and go back where they came from. I remembered the long queues of people outside the Greek Embassy in Gjirokaster. Albanians do not give up easily. They wait and wait, and persist, and try again. When I'm called forward, the immigration official gives my passport a cursory glance before handing it back. I am privileged by an accident of birth.

I walk out from the ferry terminal, round by the water. Nothing moves, no sign of life or people. At the end of the terminal approach road I turn left into the town. The streets are almost deserted. I ask a boy the way to the train station.

Dirittos and *sinistras*, fairly straightforward. Walking in these streets is pure pleasure. Sunlight slides down the stonework of the buildings and the pavement looks like cream that has been smoothed and set and left untouched. Add to this the fact that they are silent and deserted and I begin to think that this is not Italy at all but a warehouse for film props, where everyone has gone to lunch. Or an undiscovered corner of my own dreaming mind.

Then the sound of a car. Enter the first actor. He slows down when he reaches me and calls out of the open window. He wants me to speak to him, take a coffee with him, he wants...

But I don't want to play. I ignore him, he drives on, stops again, gets out – this goes on for some time – he's perfectly pleasant, says *scusi* says he's *solo*, is persistent, but eventually gives up. I walk on through the hot deserted streets. When I get to the station there's a train leaving for Rome in fifteen minutes. I buy a ticket and find the platform.

The train passes through dry, dry countryside, brown and burnt and beautiful.

Foggia, Davino, Noia, Orsara di Puglia, Savignano, Pianerottolo.

8

Marco and I walk through the stalls by the *Castel Sant'Angelo* and past the cat sanctuary and the wide-brimmed pines and we go into the *chiesa de Jesu*, all cool and trimmed with gold and there – up on the ceiling, is an angel, uncurled wings high above us – and we pass the

Pantheon and Piazza di Minerva with the elephant statue. In the via Marguta I drink from a fountain and the water runs down my arms and onto my dress. Marco takes my hand as we cross the street.

The narrow streets, all with paving and cobbles and high old buildings – other images drift in but I cannot touch these, as I can touch the stonework of the sculptures, fingered by time and the luxury of sun – so beloved is this stone, your heart shifts, turns, stretches –

In the *Biblioteca Casanatensa* there are two enormous wooden globes about three metres high. One is a map of the world, the other of the constellations. There is an exhibition of the life of Giordano Bruno, born 1548, died in Feb 1600. Because he spoke his mind and said what he thought – agreeing with Copernicus about the heliocentric nature of the solar system – he had to keep moving on. In the Cistercian order, he began in the south of Italy, went on up to Rome, then to Venice, Paris, London, Oxford, Wurtemberg and Prague, before returning to Rome. A mistake as it turned out for he was locked up for seven years and then burned at the stake. There's a statue of him in the *Campo de' Fiori*.

In the *Biblioteca* there are also woodcuts of the zodiac signs and of Mercury, Mars and Sole, pulled through the sky by their chariots. Sole and Mars have horse-drawn carriages while Mercury's is drawn by two large birds.

*

This morning we visited the *Museo Palatino*, surrounded by huge gardens, just off the *Circo Massimo*, the long grassy enclosure where they used to race chariots up and down. Elegant pines line the long avenue. The smell of the pines in the gardens of the *Palatino* was rich, dry, the smell of baked and perfumed earth.

The *Museo* has a collection of marble figures – bits of a river god's torso, a headless *inverno* draped elegantly to her feet, holding a brace of dead birds in her hand. Of *primavera* there was even less – only half of a small torso. A couple of heads – one young and the other older – of Nero, who apparently had lived here. He didn't play a fiddle, he played a harp, says Marco.

*

Last trip on the scooter. Down the hill to the *Templi di Vestia,* turning right and heading along the *Circo Massimo*, tree-lined, with the chariot runway just down below. On, heading for the arch of Titus and swinging right, with the *Colosseo* on the left, coming out into via Cavour and turning right, heading for Termini Station.

The clouds are like thin cloth, rumpled and stretched over the sky, as we arrive in Benevento. The soil here is like sand, like burnt, scorched paper. Soil and leaves are emptied of colour by the sun. The shades of soil vary from dull fawn to a brown so dark it's almost black. The leaves of the *oliviers* are grey-green, a dusty green, a smoky green. But in the trees and bushes by the embankment, in the birch leaves, there are flashes of bright yellow. I do not want to think of autumn.

*

I left Signora Maria Lista's house in the via Cairoli, Bari, early in the morning. The house had a thick wooden front door, with metal studs and a huge high-ceilinged entrance hall. Signora Lista's was on the *primo piano*. The room was spacious and high-ceilinged but very hot. Then I remembered that there was a fan in the room and that made all the difference. With a cool breeze blowing over me I soon fell asleep.

On *La Vikinga*, bound for Durres, some Italian soldiers come on board. They wear their camouflage uniform, with black berets that have two ribbons hanging down at the back. All with their regulation greeny-grey baggage.

This boat is luxury itself compared to the one I came over in. That one was like a bus, with all the seats in the middle. This one is spacious, with a café-bar at either end and plenty of seats in between. There is room to wander around, rather than be forced to remain in your seat, packed in close to other people, without room even to stretch your legs.

We're moving. *Arrivederci Italia*.

We are treated to a short video on how wonderful *Vikinga* lines are, with a demonstration of the use of life jackets and evacuation chutes – as well as life-rafts which are inflated like little yurts, little red igloos – you could imagine pleasant stewards serving you Martinis inside the red yurts.

I stand out on deck for most of the crossing. The sea is dark blue, with a tinge of purple, and a rolling muscular surface. It carries us easily on its wide blue and laughing arms. It rolls and swells and the wind grabs you like lots of hungry hands and the spray stings like soft needles. Inside, the spray is hurled against the window and the boat rolls up and down, judders a little, rolls again. My skin is slightly rough and grainy with dried salt.

9

How good too, to step off the boat and feel the very different energy of Albania. What is it about Western Europe? Their roads and pavements are so deliciously smooth, like ribbons of chocolate, that you could fold them up or so I imagine, pack them away like satin strips and lay them down somewhere else.

It makes me wonder if the slight sense of constriction I feel in Western Europe could have something to do with the roads, I don't know, but it does seem to be related to the profusion of laws and rules and regulations. Here in Albania there is an energy that just spills over all the time, there's a directness about people, a lack of self-consciousness and an affectional proximity that I really enjoy. The roads and pavements are full of potholes and broken flagstones, it's as if the energy coming up from the earth just can't be contained and held down and there is also a lack of suffocating rules and laws which make you think a lot more about what you're doing. Although this is changing, through direct Western European influence. You can no longer for example, always be certain of driving the wrong way down a one-way street with impunity. If a member of MAPE is with the Albanian policemen, you'll be fined on the spot, secure in the knowledge that the fine will not be pocketed by the policeman, but will be written down in some notebook and put away in some special place to be pocketed by someone in a higher authority.

On arrival back in Durres I found that the car that was supposed to be there to meet me had not appeared, but I was not totally surprised as communications can sometimes go wrong. A taxi driver was keen to drive me to Tirana for a mere $20 which is outrageous, so I declined and decided to walk into town and get a bus. I hadn't been walking for long when someone else who had been on the ferry caught up with me. He claimed he was Italian but was dressed like an Albanian. He was very helpful however and took me to the station where the buses leave from. We had a reasonable conversation as we walked along the dusty road, considering I only know a few words of Italian. He said he drove a lorry but this was his day off, and tomorrow he would go to Tirana. He managed to extract from me my name, age (approximate), occupation, number of children, and my reason for being in Italy. He said his name was Aqui which made me wonder if I'd found my way into a Bunyanesque morality play, with symbolic personages turning up as guides along the Way (*qui* meaning 'here' in Italian). Inhabitant of the dream-world or not, he was very kind and helpful, took me to the right minibus or *fourgon*, made sure that I got on and found a seat, and waited until it left. The journey was no more uncomfortable than the taxi would have been and cost about $1 rather than the $20 the taxi driver wanted.

This different energy has a feeling of interface and fluidity, a sense of interchangeable masks, that resist strangulation by definition and the fierce tyranny of tarmac. I also wonder if this overflowing energy of Albania has something to do with decades of oppressive communist rule that's been thrown off, so you have a people feeling an enormous sense of release. I just hope that the Western democracies don't totally succeed in imposing their culture laws and values on Balkan people because that would not suit them either – whatever evolves here needs to be their own way of doing things.

In my absence in Italy, street signs have appeared and

everywhere you go now, there are signs to tell you where you are. So I now know that I live on the Rruga Vaso Pasha for example, instead of – two blocks away from the Berliner restaurant, or one block away from the Banka Kombetare, then through the alleyway and across the courtyard, although the last part it must be said, still holds, as I don't exactly live on a street, but in a tower-block in the middle of a courtyard which is bounded on all sides by 'old' buildings. These are Russian built, dating from not long after the Second World War but look rather older. The arches out onto the main street have an Italian look to them and I think they are some of the nicest buildings in Tirana. They're only about five storeys high and I look down onto their rooftops from my balcony.

10

We drive to Elbasan to visit the Kuqan school where we are funding a programme of summer camps for the children. We go first to the Elbasan office to pick up some other people. Ylli and I are waiting in the garden in front of the office. Some of the vines woven around the trellis-work have produced plump dark grapes and I pick two and put them in my mouth.

Don't eat them, Ylli warns me, you should wash them first, otherwise you'll get sick. I make a face at him and he laughs at me. But the grape skins feel slightly thick and coated and I think maybe I should have taken his advice.

When we reach the school, I barely recognise it. I'd first seen it in winter, when there was no heating in the classrooms and the newly-planted saplings in front of the school were thin bare stalks. The saplings now look much more like young trees, covered with leaves, providing shade and protection. In a clearing in the trees a performance is taking place. A makeshift theatre has been created by draping a large cotton cloth over branches stuck in the ground. The actors are doctors who formed a theatre company specifically to help raise awareness in children of basic health issues, such as diet and hygiene. Two of the performers are dressed as bears and the third, as a stork doctor. I cannot understand the words, but the dramatic message is clear enough – one of the bears rolling on the floor, gasping and grunting, and the stork doctor appearing with his bag of tools and pulling out a stethoscope and an enormous hypodermic needle. There is a lot of laughter and the children join in, shouting encouragement or advice to bears and stork.

Afterwards, I go inside the school and in the entrance the children crowd round me, a few of them eager to practise their English. I ask them about the show, what they thought of it, what they liked. They stand around me, very close, an eager swarm of voices and suntanned faces. Then I head for a classroom to speak to some teachers. Ylli catches me in the corridor and says that the teachers and parents are waiting for me. I'll just talk to one or two I say. No, you will have to speak to them all, he says. And when I go into the room, I see it is true. They are sitting there, waiting, and I have to go to the front and address them, Ylli translating for me. I speak about the organisation and what we are doing in the summer camps and what we hope to achieve and then ask them for any comments and any problems they had.

The children have all loved it, one teacher said. And

they're already asking if we can do it again next year.

Ali Boja, whose two younger children attend the school, invites us to his house. He is a market gardener, and the porch of his house and the adjacent greenhouse, is filled with a profusion of plants. He tells us that he donated all the saplings in front of the school, to fill the bare and empty space that had been there before. In their cool, blue painted living room, his wife serves us coffee and raki, and shows us pictures of their eldest daughter, who lives in England, in Birmingham. Ali tells us how they had housed eleven Kosovar refugees, all strangers to him, the previous year. When it was time to go back, he had driven them to Kosova in his car. Like so many Albanians, he is immensely warm and generous and laughs easily. But he speaks quietly when he talks about the refugees.

Eighteen sons of one clan were killed, he said. Some were shot before their parents' eyes.

He makes us a gift of two young trees, with long feathery leaves. We drive back to Tirana with the trees sticking out of the window, trailing a green and rustling wake.

Albania Time is Very Present

We shall leave the Balkan nights behind us
the dances, the songs, the ballads, the tales
The flute alone we shall take with us
To play whenever we are homesick
Ali Podrimja

1

Autumn arrives with a *sound*, a quality of the air that carries it. It stretches it, like a torch-bearer saying – see what is beyond, further on, there is much much more, there is a quality of open door to this morning, a quality of change. It tugs at me and I want to go with it, follow it. Only I'm not sure where it would take me. I wake up at four in the morning again.

The colours of the thin clouds above Dajti mountain were deep smoky smouldering pink, before the sun rose, just above the mountain.

*

The horizon tilted, seen through an aircraft window, flown by an exhausted pilot. Or that's how it seemed to me. A mixture of exhaustion and adrenalin had thinned my skin to a porousness that let in light fever and emotion, pervasive as hallucinations. The solid – or seeming-fixed – point of reference we usually adopt as 'I' was adrift, with a flexibility imitative of sea-swell or changing landscape seen from a high altitude.

Fever gave me dreams that turned my mind into a seeming-endless computer, screen after screen opening up and making connections wildly out of my control. My mind was being fingered and stretched, speeding outwards into the vastness of space. Waking up was a relief, the exhaustion of sleeplessness far preferable to the careening night flights that felt as if I was hanging on by my fingers to an invisible vehicle that took me at the speed of light through the darkness of utterly unknown places.

We drove down to Dhermis. I saw flying fish – or skimming fish, about half a dozen of them, curving over the water surface, blades of light arching from the lip of wave. I slept out on the veranda. I saw shooting stars.

I would wake up in relief, to feel the light sea breeze on my face and the sound of the waves hissing on the creamy round pebbles of the beach. During the day I walked very slowly to the beach, lay under an umbrella, cooled off in the sea from time to time. In the evening, I walked another few meters to a restaurant table, where we all sat round, eating seafood and salad and drinking wine. The olives and tomatoes and the squares of salty cheese.

I drifted in and out of consciousness, feeling like a sea-creature floating on a gentle swell and content to be borne up by this sea which felt infinitely strong and always there, like the something that we're always looking for, that will support us and contain us and so, will set us free.

Rob diagnosed my fever as a result of stress from the

constant, driving pressure to get the USAID proposal in on time. That could account for the out-of-control computer screens my mind turned into at night, but when I opened my eyes in the morning, felt the sea air on my skin, its warmth and texture, heard the waves on the beach and the cicadas hissing, it seemed as far away from stress as I could imagine. It's cumulative, Rob said. It builds up in you over time. It's only when you stop, you realise it.

I had stopped. In the evenings Rob and I read each other extracts from a book of sea stories he'd brought with him and we laughed and played games, pretending to be other people. Then we would have competitions to see how far we could spit the water melon seeds. I would sometimes spit mine at him, pretending that my aim was really bad. This would result in wrestling matches and insults. The worst one I could think of was to call him an Australian. This would send me off into peals of laughter. One time, when we were indulging in our childish games, Olga and Chris came onto the veranda and Olga said to me severely – you must not spit seeds at him. He works for the UN, he is one of our donors. This of course only increased my laughter.

Yes, there was release of pressure here, from weight, responsibilities and deadlines. I fell in love with the pale turquoise sea as it washed through me, through my skin and through my dreams and circulated through my breath.

I knew how fickle love could be, but that was no reason not to let the sea in. I could not deny love, just because it would not always be with me. All the more reason, so it seems to me, to let it in when it comes to you, always unexpectedly, always when you're looking in some other direction, thinking that some distant horizon is where you'll see love approaching, like a ship coming to harbour.

And while I was thinking of horizons, this green sea, so full of light, lapped into me and placed a tidal pattern in my heart, so that it tugs at me, now this way, now that, like an oyster removed from its sea-bed, but still opening and closing with a tide it is no longer washed by.

This green sea is inside me now. I write with green ink and my tears are palest turquoise.

2

Back in Tirana the fever abated slightly, but the soothing sea whispers were replaced by city sounds. The blaring of car horns, the sound of builders' drills and cement mixers, the screechy rattle of steel shutters, people shouting from balconies to others in the street. Loud music emerging from shops and kiosks during the day, live music from the Berliner restaurant at night. All these sounds wove their fingers into my perceptions and sleep was light and thin as parched grass and there was rarely any breeze to shift the thick heat.

One morning I talked with François, a new colleague, about these seismic inner shifts, landslips of the psyche, the loss of ground beneath my feet and the fears like abrupt sand dunes appearing as warnings, intimations of desert.

We don't like losing our habits and predictable paths and structures in our lives, he said. Perhaps you're sensing that your life is going to change radically when you leave here. But it's creative when patterns change, because it can release blocks in you, created by fears. Do you want to be ruled by these fears?

Oh no, I say.

He then tells me that he was recently in a situation with a girl he loved and he'd decided to go away, to travel and to work abroad. His pattern, he says, is doing that. But he thought about it and decided to do something different, instead of following his usual pattern.

The fear of course is of rejection, he says, that's the only fear, after all.

So he decided to change his pattern, to say no to the job and say yes to staying and exploring the relationship – his girlfriend then turned round and said she didn't want him to stay!

But the point is, he says, now I've made that decision once and so I know that in the future it will be easier. The important thing in any relationship is what you can learn from it.

What's important is now, he says, because in two weeks time things may be very different.

He tells me of an incident that happened in India. He was there with a friend who was violently attacked and hit with clubs. Fortunately he was not badly hurt but François could not sleep for this menacing recurring image. His mind replayed it over and over again. Then, he said, he focussed on the image, gave it his full attention and the image then crystallised, like salt – went white and disappeared.

The sky has gone all thick and murky, there are rumbles of thunder and electricity and excitement in the air. A sense of lightness and liberation.

I feel desire for exploration coming back. A desire to discover and to be open to what is there and who this other place or person is. Not to know and not to have a definite picture you want this person or this place to fit into, so you can then be open to the possibilities. With no expectations it could be original, it could be itself, whatever that might be.

3

At first I loved the weather yesterday, when it rained fiercely and the sky grumbled with thunder. But later the air became chilled and my spirits dropped along with the temperature and I fell, plummeted, into an unforgiving despondency. I struggled with this as I walked along Sami Frasheri on the way back to work after lunch, turned the corner into Myslym Shyri. And on that corner and stretching further down, lined up on the pavement edge, was this array of bright colours – green and crimson peppers, yellow-green and dark blue grapes, orange cantaloupes, green and white water melons, purple aubergines, yellow bananas, bright red tomatoes, green lettuces – such a burst of colour I had to blink my eyes as I picked my way among the spreading puddles. I ran into my might-have-been landlord, the owner of the apartment I went to see with Florian. He was delighted to see me, we exchanged a few *si jne*s and he squeezed my hand so hard my ring dug painfully into my finger.

The chestnuts have fallen off the trees and lie scattered on the pavements and by the roadside. Some leaves have shrivelled and others are turning faintly yellow. There was a power cut in the apartment block and so the lift was not working. I climbed the stairs and by the second floor total darkness reigned, the same darkness you see when you close your eyes, with bursts of light and shifting areas of dim light, that do not come from outside. I climbed slowly, feeling my way with every step. I usually rely on a visual cue to tell me how many flights I've climbed – from the sixth to the seventh floor, the iron banister changes, it curves into a semi-spiral instead of being two distinct levels. But without any light at all to see by, I had to go by the feel of the steps as I lost count of how many floors I'd climbed. I thought I'd come to the eighth, but the mat outside the door did not feel right – it was a rubber one, whereas ours is a carpet. So I climbed another floor and tried the key. It worked.

On the way back down a couple of boys had a flash-light and shone it down the stairs for me, which was helpful for about three floors. Then I heard the unmistakable sounds of someone coming up and we inevitably walked straight into each other. *Me fall* (excuse me), I said and moved to one side to let him pass.

But today the sun is out again and though the wind is cool, the sun is warm on my face and feeling floods back and I love these streets again, the smaller ones turned to an ashy sludge pitted with brown puddles and the bigger ones dried, with a brown film over them and the little broken flagstones tilting unexpectedly under your feet, tipping the ball of your foot into its soggy crevice. Last night, outside the new Oslo Club just opposite Ravena's, someone had lit a small fire, the first of many that will line the winter streets. But it is not winter, it's just an unexpected cold spell. Today promises more sunshine, a warm relaxing and gentle touch of sun that will continue for many weeks before the real autumn chill sets in.

Today the woman who lives near the *pasticceria* on Abdyl Frasheri was wearing different clothes and trying on a pair of sandals. An elderly man was with her, holding a bundle of clothes and shoes. He had long white hair and pinkish trousers, tied at the waist with a cord. He had on a hat that was somewhere between the traditional white fez and a summer straw hat – a kind of creamy felt, with a well-worn look to it. I liked to think that someone was taking care of her although the sandals were too flimsy for the rough gravel, puddles and broken paving of the Tirana streets.

The steps up to the baker's have been bulldozed twice. After the first time, they carefully rebuilt them. After the second time, they've just smoothed out the rubble, so that people walk up the ramp. Their customers don't seem to mind. Their bread is good. Steps would be easier but – a stony slope will do.

4

Tirana is just one big building site, Rob said. Huge apartment blocks going up all the time. Any available space is built on, built up, going up and up, one level at a time, supported on wooden props as each level of concrete sets. There's the one at the end of Rruga Brigada, a huge edifice. Machines whine, hammers bang, and there's a faint clip-clipping sound which Rob, who is an engineer, says is a cement cutter which is used to cut concrete that's been poured somewhere it should not have been poured. My hair is damp against my neck because it's warm again.

On Sunday Rob and I went to the Art Gallery. On the first floor, I re-visited my old friends, the Socialist Realists.

Rob pointed out that in the one that showed a room full of men in suits, the perspective was wrong. On the right, but not in the foreground, you have a small group of men in lighter coloured suits. The light from a window falls on them. They have heroic looks on their faces (so you know they must be Albanian). In the foreground and on the left and even some on the same side of the table, you have men in dark suits, one of them looks like Khrushchev and they are all drawing back in gestures of protestation and disbelief. One even has an arm out to protect himself. Clearly this must have been the time of the split with Russia. But the men sitting on the same side of the table as the ones with the light encircling them like a halo are much smaller than the encirclees – though by the rules of perspective they should not have been.

According to Miranda Vickers' book *Albania* the bunkers were not built to defend Albania against invasion from the West but against invasion from Russia, who had after all, invaded Hungary and Czechoslovakia.

There are two women in the Greek shop I go into sometimes, in Rruga Bajram Curri, round the corner from my flat. One of them asked me where I was from – well I assumed that was what she asked me, as she spoke in Albanian. *Inghilterra, Scozia*, I said. The other spoke Italian and asked me where I worked. When I told her, she said that her *marito* was in *Inghilterra,* he was a Kosovar refugee, but she could not go there because she did not have the right papers, and so could not get a visa.

Rob and I talk all the time. We adopt several different personalities. He goes easily from being Robbie Blood-Axe to Robbie the Shark. He loosens up, gets into the spirit of the game. We play. We live in the present – except for moments when a slight shadow falls and we remember

I am due to leave in three weeks time – but it does not last long. Albania time is very present.

Rob phones up to say he has to go to the opening of an art gallery in Korça, funded by UNHCR on Friday and would I like to go? We could then get a lift to the Macedonian border and spend the weekend there. Oh yes, I say.

But I never reach Korça and its art gallery, or cross to Macedonia. While I thought that I still had plenty of time here to arrange a future for myself, there are forces at work in our lives that take our conscious minds by surprise. My sister phones to say my mother is critically ill in hospital and I make immediate arrangements to fly back to the UK the following day.

I pack my things, distributing some possessions among my friends. I wonder if my odd feelings of the past few days have been the responses of a deeper part of me that knew or sensed that something enormous was about to take place in my life. I remember François' words – what's important is now because in two weeks time things may be very different.

I have a farewell gathering with friends and when I come back to my apartment I stand on the balcony outside my room and look out over this city I have come to love. The evening sun paints my skin a deep reddish brown and I look down on the umbrellas of the rooftop café on the other side of Vaso Pasha.

Postscript

Ismail Kadare and the Mythic Consciousness

The town of Gjirokaster in southern Albania is the birthplace of two of its most famous sons – the Communist dictator Enver Hoxha and the writer Ismail Kadare. Enver Hoxha's former house is now a museum, a beautiful building of the Ottoman type, with polished wooden floors and ceilings, carved wooden patterns around the stairs and richly woven Albanian carpets in traditional designs and mostly in colours of red, black and undyed white.

Ismail Kadare's house, described in loving detail in his book *Chronicle in Stone,* stands open to the elements, a roofless ruin. Nothing could demonstrate more eloquently I felt, as I looked over the landscape of the city of Gjirokaster, the difference in treatment between dictator and writer, during the communist regime. The physical landscape of the city seemed to be a mirror reflection however, of the real, for Enver Hoxha's memory, as is the memory of his hated regime, has been obliterated as much as possible from people's minds, while Kadare is revered, not just in his own country, but world-wide, for his eloquent and heartfelt prose and poetry.

I'd travelled to Gjirokaster from Tirana, on a road that

bends and twists, sometimes coiling through valleys, at others climbing in serpentine loops over hills and winding down the other side, sometimes sidling up to rivers and accompanying them as if the road had followed a donkey path. It is beautiful, with views of forests and mountains, but it takes about five hours. I spent a few days there in May and it rained most of the time. Not showers or light drizzling rain, but a consistent heavy downpour. The clouds moved along the valley between the two mountain ranges, like water-bearing boats, and the rain poured steadily from them.

In *Chronicle in Stone* Kadare describes the city of Gjirokaster as being like *some prehistoric creature that was now clawing its way up the mountainside.* The setting is certainly dramatic. The buildings are perched precariously on a series of steep slopes, with a view down into the flat plain below, as if they were the audience in an amphitheatre, gazing at the stage. These stone roofed houses of Ottoman design lean out over narrow streets laid with thin cobbles, grey, yellow and pink, arranged in patterns like marble mosaics.

Kadare was born in Gjirokaster in 1936 and remembers, as he recounts in *Chronicle in Stone,* the Second World War, the dizzying changes in occupying armies (they checked the flags every morning to discover the current allegiance of their city) and the corresponding changes in the nationalities of the aerial bombardments. He attended secondary school in Gjirokaster, a building of Italian design, where today there is a plaque on the wall, commemorating his attendance. He later studied at Tirana University and the Gorky Institute in Moscow and became known in the West after his novel *The General of the Dead Army* was translated into French. His output

209

is prodigious, his work has been translated into many languages, and many of them are now available in English.

Kadare's writing is full of the power of the mythic consciousness, not just as some remembered stories from some distant era, but as it affects us here and now in our lives, whenever that 'now' may happen to be, whether in 1389 on the plain of Kosovo, in the 15th century in northern Albania, or 21st century Tirana.

It has been said of the people of the Balkans that the past is very present for them, there is not such a clear line of demarcation between them, and so, that time is understood more mythologically rather than chronologically. But this mythological understanding or experience of time, is also one that is shared by poets and other creative people and could be said to reflect an awareness of the larger dimensions of reality. It is quite astonishing, then, that someone of Kadare's sensibility could have managed not only to survive under a repressive communist regime, but to have also written and published such great works of fiction that Kadare produced. As he says in his introduction to *Albanian Spring*,

The writer is the natural enemy of a dictatorship...The writer submits to only one law, that of Art. In this way, he lives in a sense, outside of time.

His survival however, was not an easy one. More than once, his writing was attacked under one pretext or another. In communist Albania an attack on your writing was tantamount to saying that you were critical of the government, potentially a very dangerous position to be in.

I had no idea, when I looked down at the ruin of Kadare's house, that a few weeks later I would meet the man who had lived there and described the house, the streets, the occupants and the bombardments and chaos of World War II, in *Chronicle in Stone*. But, through a mutual friend, I acquired an invitation to visit him in his apartment on the Left Bank.

The massive wooden doors of the apartment block lead into an inner courtyard. When I close the doors behind me, all the noise of the busy Paris street outside is blocked off. A second door leads to a huge wooden staircase, varnished, carpeted, and thick with silence.

I ring the doorbell and Ismail Kadare opens it. I recognise him instantly from photographs but I'm surprised at his youthful appearance. It seems hardly credible that this is someone who had lived through World War II. We go through the hallway to a large elegant living-room, with pale yellow sofas and armchairs, varnished wooden floor and a patterned rug of rich dark colours.

When I ask him about the importance to him of the Greek myths, which figure in his writing, he says it is very important to know about the Greek tragedies because the Greek myths, the Greek consciousness, 'that is the reality which shapes our lives. This is true for everyone' he says, 'not just the peoples of the Balkans,' though he admits that the past and the present are very close for the Balkan people and so the past there is particularly alive.

We then talk about his book *Albanian Spring* (*Printemps Albanais*). The book covers the events that took place in Albania from the early months of 1990 to the autumn of that year. It is as much a chronicle of Kadare's own path and part in these events, with his intimate involvement with his own destiny as well as that of his country, for he shows clearly how closely the two are intertwined. His love for his country is as apparent as his pain at the decision to leave. He outlines the unfolding events that have the resonance of the Greek tragedies with which he is so familiar. We feel Necessity, the Fates, and the whispers of the Erinyes stalking the streets of Tirana.

These events include the brief 'spring' that gives the book its title – a three week period in May of that year, where some democratic changes were made and the possibility of freedom and respect for human rights hovered like a mirage. That 'spring' was a direct product of Kadare's intervention, his speaking out against abuses and violations of human rights and his championing of the cause of freedom.

The second part of the book contains a transcript of the long letter he wrote to Ramiz Alia, the then President, as well as his reply. It outlines Kadare's profound concerns, particularly about the violation of human rights, and cites some examples of abuses suffered by individuals. These examples give us a glimpse of what it must have been like for people living under such a regime, with its unpredictable attacks, cruelties and penalties, when you had no recourse to any real justice. It was not a letter to which he expected a reply, but when the reply did come, it was clear that the brief 'spring' was over. The mechanisms of dictatorship returned, like an addiction that it could not break. Because of that, Kadare made his decision to leave, in the belief that, by this action, and his absence, he could be more effective.

This book is necessary reading for anyone wishing to understand what was happening in Albania during this vital period of change, from the point of view of someone who was both influencing it and living through it, as well as for an understanding of Kadare's own actions and decisions during this time. From his description in *Printemps Albanais*, the decision to leave his country, which he loved, was not taken lightly; on the contrary, it went against his deepest desires. Far from being self-seeking, looking only to his own safety, it was more self-sacrificing, believing that his absence could help his country more than his presence. It is interesting to note that shortly after he left Albania the dictatorship did begin to crack and eventually fall apart. More than a decade after these events, Kadare now spends about six months of the year in Albania.

When I leave, he walks back with me down the long carpeted hall of his apartment. We stop in front of the door. At the end of the hall there's a framed black and white photograph on the wall. It's of an old Albanian man, his smiling face creased and lined with age and life's experiences. It's a face vivid with life and emotion, the eyes wide open and direct, gazing at you. On his head he is wearing a white fez, typical of Albanians of the north, and he is smoking a cigarette.

'Taken during the war,' Kadare says, and stops and gazes at it with obvious affection.

Back outside in the busy Paris street, jammed with people and the noise of traffic, I feel as if I have come from some Olympian heights where tranquillity and a profound moral authority reigns, into the chaos of the modern marketplace of central Paris. Yet some of the atmosphere has rubbed off and stayed with me, this peculiar magic of a slight and quiet-spoken person who lives both within his own historical time and that other time where myth guides our footsteps and our actions.

I remembered when I was in Gjirokaster, I went with my hosts one evening up a twisting road even higher than the Ottoman fortress, visiting people living in one of the oldest inhabited houses. When we came out, thunder and lightning illuminated the valley and the city, turning it into the essence of drama, with the eerie greenish light and the loud thunder right over our heads, as we stood in the garden, high up on top of the world it seemed, with a steep drop below into nothingness. We carefully negotiated the steps curving round to the path that would lead us back to the track, our way illuminated from time to time by the lightning flashes.

Gjirokaster is very close to the border with Greece, the homeland of the gods, so it hardly then seems surprising that Jupiter, god of lightning bolts, should perform with such drama and vigour – he was in his home territory after all. Not surprising either, that living in such close proximity to the land of origin of these timeless myths should have a profound influence on your psyche. Is this I wondered, why the Balkan peoples experience time as mythological? Is there an energy in the land itself that feeds them with a sense of timelessness as well as Everyday? The Greek myths are the reality 'that have shaped and ordered all our lives' Kadare had said. On the mountain top at Gjirokaster, walking carefully down dark stone steps slippery with rain, the lightning throwing its shadowless glare over the heavy roofed house, the tangled foliage and the garden ending in a precipice, I had no doubt that it was true.

(This article was first published in *The Dublin Quarterly* in 2006 http://www.dublinquarterly.ie/07/ft_msmith.html)

Further Reading

Lord Byron, *Childe Harold's Pilgrimage*
Robert Carver, *The Accursed Mountains: Journeys in Albania*
Edith Durham, *High Albania*
Robert Elsie (ed), *An Elusive Eagle Soars: Anthology of Modern Albanian Poetry*
Ismail Kadare, *Chronicle in Stone*
Tessa de Loo, *In Byron's Footsteps*
Fatos Lubonja, *Second Sentence*
Noël Malcolm, *Kosovo: A Short History*
Miranda Vickers and James Pettifer, *Albania: From Anarchy to a Balkan Identity*

Morelle Smith's travel blog:
http://rivertrain.blogspot.co.uk